My Ordinary Life

My Ordinary Life

Poems by Franklin Abbott

RFD PRESS

v. 25-0104

ISBN 979-8-9876654-2-8

9 798987 665428

Library of Congress Control Number: 2025904923

cover calligraphy by Franklin Abbott,
cover design by Thomas West
and the photo on the back cover by Bob Burkhardt

in memory of my parents

Jack F. Abbott and
Mildred Carpenter Abbott

INTRODUCTION

The center is still and silent in the heart of an eternal dance of circles.

— Rabindranath Tagore

Life is full of circles. Just before the curtain dropped when Covid emerged on the world stage as a killer, I had been in India visiting friends and giving a talk at a college. Less than a week ago with travel relatively safe again, I returned to Atlanta, my home town, after two months in India visiting friends and places I had visited on my last trip (2019) and my first trip (2007) and going to places that have lived long in my imagination. It was like a movie, literally. Lots of bumpy roads, lots of waiting and tedium for those golden moments that are spliced into memory, as what we hold and cherish as precious.

My father died a year and some months ago. After his death and the lifting of the pall of Covid, I decided to retire. I had worked in human services for more than fifty years and in private practice as a licensed clinical social worker for over forty. When I made the decision I had trepidation about such a big change. When I made the change a burden was lifted. I did not feel the regret I thought I would. I felt light as a feather. I could feel my wings again and so I flew back to India. I had friends and places to fly to and complete the circles that had been spinning for years and decades. I had not realized how poignant my longing had become. I missed the colors, the noise, the insistence of being. Everywhere I journeyed the insistence of being was waiting for me speaking a dozen different languages, calling out to me in temples, palaces, kitchen tables, street life and nature sanctuaries.

My experiences were woven into a cloak, a coat of many vibrant colors. When I wrap it around me I feel both safe and elegant, both rich and replete. I am a rickshaw driver on the road to the village and the wealthy modern maharaja, my feet don't touch the ground. Being human I am vulnerable to both loneliness and fatigue. One doesn't cancel the other out. What to call that hollow place between earth and sea? My friend Souryadeep is tuning his sarod, my friend Raju is tightening the strings of his khemak, my friend Ankur is inviting me to sing. All the Boro people are there, I am given a crimson scarf and asked to sing a poem. Every year in spring . . . I sing.

These story poems offered here are divided into three sections. The first are scattered poems I wrote before Covid. The last of these are the poems I wrote about India whose door closed just a few months after I left. The middle section, most of the poems, were composed during Covid and I could not create a meaningful chronology because there was none. Covid was back and forth, topsy turvy, congealed and falling apart. So are the poems in this section. The last poems are post-Covid, if there is such a thing. I want to believe there is. I want to believe that we are free and safe again, at least from a lurking deadly virus.

The Covid times came with gifts. I had to slow down, way down and that allowed me to pay attention to things I would have missed in my hurried life. Each interaction became more special. Things I had to give up became more valuable (or not) when I could have them again. Grief and Fear were constant companions and yet the sweetness of life continued to permeate my days and nights. Being very careful and very fortunate I did not and have yet to contract Covid. But I suffered from collateral damage as we all did. Important events were sacrificed, the ability to move, to reach out to friends in need, to share meals, attend concerts . . . There were many losses and much grief, so much grief it was hard to feel it all. It will take years to come to terms with the profound losses of people and safety and calm.

Most of the poems in this collection are as much stories as they are poems. I could call them story poems because there is a little story in each of them. Covid coincided for me with the last years of my parents' lives. They did not die from Covid but during and just after. It was also a time when I was reckoning with my own aging and that of many of my closest friends. And it was a time of tempest and woe in the world, something that has not abated as conflicts intensify and our environment becomes more hazardous. Maybe one of the odd gifts of living through a pandemic is to take joy where we can find it. Stress is heavy and worry takes a toll. And yet little moments of sweetness and light break through and we can still find delight.

My hope for my readers is that my stories help you remember your own and that you share them whether in written form, as art, music or conversation across a shared meal. The novelist Isak Dinesen said that all sorrows can be borne if you put them into a story. Here are some of mine and I offer them as an invitation for you to share yours. I hope this book can be a friend, a comfort and an assurance that you are not alone.

Franklin Abbott
23 February 2025
Atlanta

ACKNOWLEDGEMENTS

The work of the mature person is to carry grief in one hand
and gratitude in the other and to be stretched large by them.
 – Francis Weller

The poems that became this book were written largely
over the past four years and circulated via email to friends
and family. The responses that I received were a great
source of encouragement in navigating the difficult days
of Covid lockdown, the diminishment and deaths of
both of my parents, the loss of dear friends, and my own
concerns as I aged into my seventies. Many of these
people are mentioned by name in the poems and many
are not. There is no intention to leave anyone out. The
poems simply rose from my experiences. I do want to
acknowledge the support I received from my brother and
sister-in-law in relation to our parents. They helped me
bear the grief and took on the lion's share of responsibility.
I received a great deal of support from dear friends close by
and far afield. They listened and reached out. We often
shared grief and as often shared gratitude. I am grateful
to live in overlapping communities, some defined by my
neighborhood and some by Internet connections, where,
again I have received support and immense kindness.

I have had the help of healthcare professionals, my doctors,
dentist, chiropractor, acupuncturist, physical therapists.
These brave individuals continued to do the work of helping
and healing even when we were behind masks and taking
calculated risks. Likewise all the essential workers who
delivered goods, stocked grocery store shelves, drove me
to the airport, helped me care for my home and my animal

companions. It is hard to feel gallant doing ordinary things but there was as much gallantry in the face of a deadly virus as there would be on any battlefield. I can hold the grief of all the loss in part because of the gratitude I experience. I am grateful, very grateful that I can say thank you.

With the mechanics of the book I am grateful to Tom West who has done a great job designing the book and helping me with lots of logistics. I am grateful to my dear friend and fellow poet, Don Perryman, for his precise attention to editorial detail. I thank my publicist Michele Karlsberg and publisher Brian Schwartz for their good help and guidance. I am grateful for the support of my friends at RFD Press, Bambi Gauthier and Matt Bucy for their support. I offer advance gratitude to my readers who are moved to share the book with their friends and family. May we hold tight through times of tension and uncertainty knowing it is always better when we are generous and kind.

One last thank you to the Lillian E. Smith Center in Clayton, Georgia. Lillian E. Smith was white civil rights advocate in the early days of the modern civil rights movement. A close friend of Martin Luther King, Jr. and an educator and publisher whose own books, Strange Fruit and Killers of the Dream, are classics of controversy. She ran a camp for girls with her life partner, Paula Snelling, with whom she edited and published South Today. The center houses a museum for Lillian's books and memorabilia. The meditation garden pays homage to the school and to Lillian and Paula who are buried there. The cottages for artists are full books and artifacts from Lillian's family. I stayed as a guest and resident several times. The peace of the mountain and the palpable soul of Lillian gave me the strength and comfort to edit this manuscript. Homage to the staff and to the deep hum of the forest.

ENDORSEMENTS

Franklin's writing is anything but ordinary. Like many of the great storytellers, he utilizes everyday occurrences as an opportunity to explore the phenomenon of aging. In this book, Franklin vulnerably shares what happens when life forces us to slow down and sit with ourselves—what materializes when we painstakingly pivot ourselves to just being without the familiarity of always doing. In these poems and stories, Franklin bridges the human experience across literal continents and shifting states of mind, centering how we embody memories, pain, grief, connections and joy.

> – **Dr. Luis R. Alvarez-Hernandez,** *Professor at Boston University and author of "See Me! Gay and Trans Latinos' Testimonios on Mental Health, Discrimination, and Joy in South Texas"*

The first poem that attracted me to the oeuvre of Franklin Abbott's fascinating poetry was a celebration of the ordinary everyday food in India eaten by the rich and the poor. Of course it was born of his Indian connection as he ate the humble Dal, which he says goes far beyond the lentil cooked abroad. He goes onto savour the spices, flavours and aromas that go into it's making. And as one goes through his poems in his latest collection 'My Ordinary Life', one is amazed at his turning the ordinary, which forms much of human existence, in such a reachable yet extraordinary way. Yet another poem that touches one deeply is titled, 'The News is Often Unbearable' as he sits with his friends in his country with his two friends , one from India and one from Pakistan, in the backdrop of 'mass shootings, senseless wars'. Yet the three friends create memory of sitting together and eating their dinner in peace. Such is the soothing balm of the poet from poem to poem in this memorable collection.

> – **Nirupama Dutt,** *author of The Ballad of Bant Singh: A Qissa of Courage*

At the peak of the AIDS epidemic, Franklin Abbott created many compelling, memorable poems about love and desire in a time of catastrophe — some of which have lingered close to my heart through the years. His last book, *My Ordinary Life*, speaks about survival during another pandemic: the one caused by the recent coronavirus. The sense of urgency is here less prevalent, for time has passed and this pandemic carried, evidently, different challenges. A critical question, however, remains: how is it possible to live "ordinarily" throughout devastation, uncertainty, and confinement? In a time of social distance, this book demonstrates that each moment of sanity can become a small victory. In this sense, Franklin Abbott's snippets of "ordinary life" are anything but ordinary: they underscore the value of those things in life we take for granted — and they do so beautifully, with an elegant, unpretentious verse that speak to the reader warmly, like an embrace coming from a time in which we were not allowed to hug others. That is, in the end, the magic of words: they can fill the voids, nourish in times of scarcity. By displaying the poems in alphabetical order, Abbott distorts the idea of time passing —which brings back that sense of stasis many of us experienced during lockdown— and invites the reader to meander through the pages, with the joy that stems from a hopeful heart.

– **Isaias Fanlo,** *Professor at University of Cambridge, author of the novel El pes de la boira*

Franklin Abbott's 'My Ordinary Life' is a paean to the ordinary life. Written in confessional mode, the poet finds in the ordinary, his own life as well as the lives of others. This is the life of weather, of friends alive and departed, of good food on the table when the news outside wearies you. It is the life of love, and it is as simple as sitting together. This brings acceptance to things, which brings peace. The poet writes about 'growing older/ letting go/ and opening up/about the wisdom of cats/the symphony of nature/ and the mute display of flowers/ in my garden'. Elsewhere, he finds that 'time is the rice/we pour the sauce upon…/and sip by sip/ life has coaxed us/to live another day'. These existential ruminations in plainspeak try to find what is often overlooked. While writing elegies for friends, the poet discovers that there is nothing extraordinary about death either, which too comes as a matter of course, leaving the remembered life incandescent.

– **Amlanjyoti Goswami,** *author of A Different Story*

In *My Ordinary Life*, Franklin Abbott offers readers the reflective rarity of being human—a sojourn marked by cycles of loss and renewal, grief and gratitude, isolation and connection. Through the prism of ordinary days shaped by extraordinary times, Abbott explores glints of humanity that exist in every moment of our own being—whether at the kitchen table, in a pantheon, or the realm between the sea and land. His creations—born of pandemic solitude, the loss of loved ones, and the curve balls of life—reveal the intrinsic spiritual reward woven through our daily existence and enriched through acts of kindness, the sharing of experiences, and the resiliency found in community. Abbott reminds us that even in the shadow of uncertainty, sweet and shining moments persist, and that when carrying grief in one hand and gratitude in the other, the arc of humanity is stretched and capable of finding meaning, comfort, and belonging as the Lachesis of ordinary people who live extraordinary lives.

> – **Maurice J. Hobson, Ph.D.,** *Historian, Social Scientist, Africana Studies Scholar, Producer, and Social Justice Champion; Author of The Legend of the Black Mecca: Politics and Class in the Making of Modern Atlanta (2017) and With Faith in God and Heart and Mind: A History of Omega Psi Phi Fraternity (2025).*

What an amazing collection this is! It defies genre: memoir, travelogue, meditation, prose and poetry, ode and ballad, lyric and anecdote, all at the same time. A celebration-of-age story. A tribute to people the writer has known, loved, or come across. An elegy to all that was precious, and remains so, now only in memory. Those little incidents of life. The humdrum. The plain, everyday happenings. Encounters, engagements, cares, considerations. Mundane rituals of life. The penance and joys of living. In Franklin Abbott's gentle hands, unadorned and unembellished, they become consecrated, grace and service.

The gift of wisdom. Gratis and ungrudging. Exemplary, the economy of these poems. The art of spare, plain expression. The gradations, scale, and spectrum of feelings and emotions it is fine-tuned to convey. Poetry, nonetheless, that seems to come as naturally as the morning breeze. And what could be a higher form of imagination than that which turns the ordinary events of daily life into the most magical experiences? Franklin Abbott's *My Ordinary Life* launches, in my view, a major new voice in modern American poetry. A collection for the ages.

> – **Waqas Khwaja,** *Ellen Douglass Leyburn Professor of English Agnes Scott College and author of "Hold Your Breath" and "No One Waits for the Train"*

What a gift Franklin Abbott gives us with this new collection! These story-poems talk of life, illness, friendship, food, aging, travel, and death in profoundly honest ways. Shuttling nimbly between the spiritual and the mundane, it is in his word choices and line breaks that Abbott most ably shows us his brilliance as a mature poet (and human being). For those of us who are already fans, we know how his poems have brightened dark roads and lessened the burdens of the last decades. In these perilous times, we need these new verses more than ever.

> – **Cary Alan Johnson,** *author of Desire Lines*

By personal experience, training, and as a practicing therapist for many decades, Franklin Abbott has gained and shared deep insights into human thinking and behavior. In *My Ordinary Life*, his third book of poems, he has used lucid and lyrical phrasing to apply this valuable awareness to his own life and the lives of many others he's known and loved in recent years. My first reaction on hearing his new title was that this life, even in its simplest daily minutiae, has been anything but ordinary. I'm confident that anyone who learns about it in these pages will agree.

> – **Don Perryman,** *author of the poetry collection, Hearts Bigger than Brazil*

In My Ordinary Life, Franklin Abbott not only recreates the quotidian but casts contemplative glances backward and forward. Readers will journey alongside the poet as he navigates the loss of both aged parents, his own physical and psychic pain, and dislocations caused by covid. The gift Abbott shares is his enduring understanding that "in the love of life / is its ache.

    – **Steven Riel,** *Author of Edgemere*

In My *Ordinary Life*, poet and psychotherapist Franklin Abbott offers a quietly profound meditation on the poignancy of the human condition, told through lyrical story-poems that transform ordinary moments into small altars of insight and revelation. With a voice both wise and vulnerable, Abbott finds poetry in the fabric of daily life—shared meals with friends, ancestral memories, investigations of aging and loss, late-night reflections, and travels across the globe. His writing is spacious yet intimate, deeply personal yet unmistakably universal. More than a memoir, My *Ordinary Life* is a tender, unflinching portrait of a life attentively lived. It speaks across generations, and diverse audiences, offering a powerful reminder and inspiration to live life fully, with presence, grace, and open-hearted clarity.

    – **Harvey L. Schwartz, Ph.D.,** *author of Dialogues with Forgotten Voices and The Alchemy of Wolves and Sheep*

My *Ordinary Life* is full of family and friends, dying and living, mourning and celebrating, eating and drinking — in short — it is full of life.

    – **Alice Teeter,** *author of Here, at the end*

CONTENTS

everyday I live my ordinary life so lovely so rich and so sweet it doesn't seem to matter how it repeats itself over and over goes round and round where its been to where its going everyday I live my ordinary life so lovely so rich and so sweet it doesn't seem to matter how it repeats itself over and over goes round and round where its been to where its going everyday I live my ordinary life so lovely so rich and so sweet it doesn't seem to matter how it repeats itself over and over goes round and round where its been to where its going everyday

Prologue

THE SEATED MUSICIAN

the final terracotta figure in the exhibition
was called "the seated musician"
this young man was sitting on the ground
his legs fully extended
he was holding an instrument that had
long since turned to dust
probably a stringed instrument
he would pluck or play with a bow
his face was unlike the faces of the others –
infantrymen, generals, bureaucrats
his features were soft, his expression, tender
you understand he played his zither
not just with his hands
but with his dulcet spirit
when he returned my gaze
with a shy smile
I held my breath to hold the moment
and then he turned back into clay
waiting two thousand years to play
for his dead emperor
buried in a vast necropolis
while China became China
just above his head

LANIER'S LAST TURN

Sam, the night nurse
Nigerian/Ibo
had midwifed death before
Sam said turn him
he said in dying we become rigid
and so need to be turned
there was an orange towel
on the bed under Lanier
I pulled in the direction
Sam told me to pull
Roger, Lanier's nephew
gathered pillows
to arrange for maximum comfort
Sam turned Lanier to the side
where Roger and I sat
Rainbow Moon pulled in a chair
and sat with us in between
she turned to me and said,
"I haven't blown you off
about the gourd books."
I understand why
she had been here
and would be here
until the end
Rainbow Moon
had midwifed death before
we chatted about gourds
and I told her
of meeting
the Gourd Woman of Wrens
the Friday before
and had made the mistake

of asking
how she got into gourds
we laughed as she told us the story
of how she had gotten into gourds
Lanier was breathing deeply
listening to us
like we were windchimes
in his heart
Lanier loved the sounds
of conviviality

another radical philosopher
Stephen Levine once told me
we die as we live
to steady me on my way home
I shook Sam's hand
before I left
I tossed and turned before Nancy
left me a message just before
I woke up
and then I fell into a deep sleep

Nancy told me she went in
to kiss Lanier good night
and his breathing was changing
becoming more spacious
Sam told her to get Pauline

surrounded by love
in his home
under his most vivid painting
Lanier died
as he lived
his last breath

a sigh of release
his last breath
a sigh of release
his last breath
a sigh of release

in memory of R. Lanier Clance

SHARON'S SUITCASE

she had told me about the suitcase
and I had pictured something old-timey
maybe brown leather with gold initials embossed
a leather handle and buttons that would pop open
with the turn of a tiny key
but it was much more modern
more like a backpack on wheels
red and black
it was in front of the blue file cabinet
in the office that was closed to the cats
the housekeeper said she did vacuum that room
to keep her smell she said as she opened the door
smell she said, can you smell her?

she showed me the white box that held my friend's remains
we talked about the oxygen machine that was brand new
at rest in the corner and maybe could be donated
I was provided with boxes and a trash can
my job was to empty the blue file cabinet
I rolled out the suitcase first
it took up more than space
it seemed to have a life of its own
just barely breathing

I thought my friend would be more organized
she was a one two three kind of person
the alphabet was important to her
she was an English teacher among other things
but personal files were mixed with tax returns
one was a file with her wife's name on it
her wife was in the other room

I took it to her
she looked inside
and seemed surprised
"she kept everything."

it didn't take more than an hour to sort the personal
and the old receipts
to find the program for her father's memorial
and her mother's will
to fill the trash can with all that didn't matter
and put what did in the box
that will go with the suitcase
to the archive
where this writer's life
that couldn't be saved
will not be lost

in memory of Sharon Sanders

MY PARENTS, 91 AND 92

when I say they are becoming invisible
it is not in space
they are not translucent becoming transparent
it is in sound
where what was words is becoming breath
it is in time
where the minutes are expanding, stretching
you can see through the hours
the horizon is foggy, incoherent
and through the haze
the smoke of burning calories
the vapor of rising waters
the kiss of steam
from the kettle on full throttle
there is nothing but the future
what is past is over
what is now
is evaporating
slowly hissing itself
out of existence

HARRY AND JOHN

John was sweet
to Harry's sour, salt
to Harry's pepper
taken together
they were quite a dish

in memory of Harry Hay and John Burnside

Mamaw —
My Mother's Mother

my grandmother told me the story
of her name when I asked who for
or how she was named Christine
Christine was the 13th of 14
for her father and the 9th of 10
for her mother
her older brother Lesslie
died of influenza before
the close of the First World War
her closest sister Amalta
became a grand diva
of the Eastern Star of Alabama
and married the Postmaster
of Birmingham even though
they lived in Alabaster
and died childless
which is why I sit on her
horsehair overstuffed Victorian sofa

my grandmother told me
she had gone with her mother
to the factory where she worked
where she was sat outside
to wait and not move
when the woman she was named for
a friend of her mother's
stopped in front of her
and asked the question
do you know who I am?
I asked her

if she did and what
did she say
(she was only 6 or 7)
she looked at me
with her cow brown eyes
without blinking
and told me plain:
I spit in
her face

by the time of our conversation
her Parkinson's Disease made help
necessary for everything manual
I fed her now just like she fed me
when I was tiny
I held the straw to her mouth
while she suckled a vanilla milkshake
I'd brought with the onion rings
she loved from the Sonic Drive-In

I always cried afterwards
alone in the elevator
of McKendree Manor
but while we were together
only smiled
as she smiled back at me
happy for the next bite
the next sip
and the next salutation

between the spiteful child
and the grateful elder
a life worn smooth
and round as a stone
in the bed
of a mountain brook

in memory of Christine Watson Carpenter
The Order of the Eastern Star is the women's auxiliary of the Freemasons.

LOSING IRMA LEE

a gestalt poem

her brown eyes were confusing
she was so much water
she was aquamarine amniotic
you could be a tadpole swimming
inside her grace
when you looked into her eyes
the earth looked back at you
when she closed her eyes at last
you cried and fell down
on the earth
that held you
gently
like she did
when you knew you
had to let go
and didn't want to
completely

in memory of Dr. Irma Lee Shepard

METAMORPHOSIS

I had to give up
the mulberry tree
that hung over
the driveway
(no silk woven here)
all the same
the taste of ripe
mulberries
silkened my soul
I had to give up
the smell of dirt
in the cellar
the towering transplanted
bitter cane
the worm
of my imagination
became a butterfly
and flew
away

THE DREAM EGG

every morning I have to peck my way out
of the dream egg

I raise my weary head and tighten my beak how many
pecks, how many pecks until the shell cracks and a tiny eye
of light appears, how many pecks, how many pecks until
the eye becomes a sliver of the day: now I move my feet,
my tiny feet that do not know this day I peck and push,
peck and push until a door opens and more light than
my eyes my dreaming eyes, just barely open, can bear to
see, streams through the door in the egg I push and roll and
peck and roll, I strain to see in the blinding light the world
is a roar of sound and the sun of the world blinds me

I close my eyes and open my eyes
close my eyes and open my eyes
I roll til one foot is under my body
I stretch my wet wings
I make a peep
I roll and stretch until free of the shell
I roll and stretch til the shell falls away
I push and stretch to get on my feet
I push and stretch and stand
and shake my head
and shake my yolk soaked wings

I am walking slowly around in a circle
I am seeing colors and forms emerge from the brightness

16

I am hearing my own peep, peep in the roar of the world
I am breathing a sigh of relief
though I cannot yet fly I can sigh
The shell of the dreamworld is broken
the dream of the egg is vanishing in the bright light
I can feel my feet and hear my heart beat
the light of the world is drying my feathers
somewhere from deep within I hear the beginning
of the song I will sing today

India 2019

Thane

if I were dreaming
and I walked into a room
of Laxmi's and Saraswati's
I would be unable to speak
when I was told where to sit
and offered refreshments

I had a proctor
Professor Pandey
she is of small stature
but big presence
and thirty years my junior
and she became my ruler

always taking me away
from students wanting selfies
to my next official
engagement
I noticed the other honorees
not so sheparded
she made sure
I showed up

what I enjoyed most
was eating in the canteen
where the food was good what we might deem
wholesome
my philosopher colleagues
Einstein and Sartre

fingers dripping with dal
and my tepid disclosure
I don't seem to be able
to use my fingers
to hold the naan
to dip the dal

Professor Pandey
looked me
eye to eye
and said
we have been doing this
since we were children

Gurgaon

islands of marble
courtyards of the greenest grass
near nothing
not culture
not family
sidewalks broken into bits
straydogs of the district hunkered on corners

hard to heat in Winter
morning tea
a solace

I love my friend
and have come to love
her family
her sisters go with us to a craft market
each gifts me with a small bronze statue

they are of one mind
both the Buddha and Lord Ganesha
are reclining
her niece and nephew
take me for a romp in Old Delhi
I eat forbidden foods
forget to wash my hands
eat again in a posh restaurant
in Connaught Street
and doze off
on the long road back
to Gurgaon

Lucknow

my young friend
was going to an academic conference
in Lucknow, fabled Oudh
and so we met at the Delhi airport
and sat in the last seats
in the back of the plane
leaning in
we decided on three sites
for our day of sightseeing
the Imambara, the Residency
and the new Ambedkar Memorial
by the time we got to the third
my friend was leading me up the stairs
and the plaza with its regiment of giant elephants
surrounded us like water
so how could we not look up
the sky was becoming a rose
we found our way back

to our hotel
and took a walk
and ate roasted peanuts
which my friend could
crack and cull
with incredible skill
and put a few warm nuts in my hand
easy for me
to eat
and want more

Assam

so when my Facebook friend Parag
invited me to visit Assam
he said I am poor but stay in my house
and I replied I do not want to inconvenience you
I can stay in a hotel
and he said no stay in my house

he met me at the Guwahati airport
just as the sun was setting
he was riding a scooty
and assigned the best English speaking member
of his family to ride with me in the taxi
she being 13 and knowing hello and how are you
we drove away from the city lights
down miles of highway
and turned off onto a darker narrow road
and after miles
turned into a dirt driveway
and through a bamboo gateway
into a courtyard
lit by a single light bulb

his mother had made tea
and a simple dinner
we ate together
under the light of one bulb
and I slept in a bamboo house
with a tin roof on top
and in the morning I heard
the eggs of my breakfast
being laid with a loud cluck
and the milk of my morning
still warm with the moo
of the cow

everyday I live my ordinary life so lovely so rich and so sweet it doesn't seem to matter how it repeats itself over and over goes round and round where its been to where its going everyday I live my ordinary life so lovely so rich and so sweet it doesn't seem to matter how it repeats itself over and over goes round and round where its been to where its going everyday I live my ordinary life so lovely so rich and so sweet it doesn't seem to matter how it repeats itself over and over goes round and round where its been to where its going everyday

My
Ordinary Life

AFTER HOURS

I had shut off the TV
after watching the BBC news
and my father came rambling
back into the room
saying he couldn't sleep
so we talked for an hour
about my mother
his not yet dead a year wife
and his long dead parents
and even longer dead grandmother
Mother Gable
who he claims hated him
because he outdistanced her favorites
his uncle and his sister

my father, now 93
is focused on his maladies
a bladder that can't hold
a knee that gives out
and a mind that won't remember
no matter how much sudoku he does

between sympathy
and exasperation I vascillate
but tonight my body has relaxed
and my mind massaged by PBS
I listen and respond

like he will remember our conversation
and not repeat repeat repeat
I believe rapport makes a difference
when he feels like someone is listening
or noticing if with strain he can draw
the blinds shut
he becomes more genial
more like someone who is someone
which is something we don't want age
to rob us of
we are still someone
maybe we can't remember
or repeat ourselves
maybe it takes three times longer
to draw down the shades
maybe we are telling a story
for the thirty-third time
but we are someone
who has a heart beat
who breathes in and breathes out
who has preferences and opinions
and capabilities

my father proudly drove his car
a mile and a half to a gas station
where if you pull up in the inside lane
someone will check the pressure in your tires
and fill up your tank
and more remarkably
he drove home and parked in his garage

his caregiver made hamburgers for supper
she reads articles in magazines
about recipes
she made good peanut butter cookies
earlier today
but cooking is work for her
I appreciate she cooks for my father

I told her I would teach her how to
pan fry fish tomorrow
I can fry fish in my dreams

my head is bending
like a flower who's bloom is spent
I will lie down soon
I have paid my rent

my father is asleep in the room next
I hope he has sweet dreams, children who don't
wake him but guide him
to the Good Ship Lollypop

ALL THE SPACE
IN A CHINESE PAINTING

after six psychotherapy sessions
and still rebalancing after a talk at GSU
and minor surgery the day before
and a knee that aches
having gotten my ducks in a row
for tomorrow
my friend Kilian arrives to take me to dinner
and we go around the corner for Mexican
in Oakhurst
Kilian doesn't drink but suggests I do
a Margarita for my knee
and I drink
I like salt and lime and tequila

our rapport is such
that we often order the same thing
I'll have what he's having
when our order came out
I asked the server to make sure
I didn't get his
she had two plates
of the same food
she looked slightly confused
he said you got her
it was congenial
and so we ate the same food
and talked about his film projects
including his first movie
and we talked about my travels
to Washington, DC

and how my knee
felt the pavement
every step of the Lincoln Memorial
and we talked about his family
and got back to my house for tea
and we talked about my family
and how hard it is to know what you want
and to make art out of life
and the cats were tired
who knows how many strays
they warded off
the blinds were askew
and they listened
one eye open
as we talked about knowing
what they always know
they always know what they want

Kilian had brought in a small white trunk
he didn't want to leave in his van
inside the trunk were special lenses
more valuable than both of our cars
put together
in another country we would not have
the front door open
and he would not carry this treasure
from his van without an armed guard
and my house would be inside a gate
that was inside a gate
but he carried the small white trunk
without incident
and I without incident
closed the door slowly
and the cats without incident
lounged on the couch

and in an overstuffed chair
and the night became quiet
my knee stopped beeping
and in just a few strokes
I will stop typing
and set myself to dreaming
about the poem of tomorrow
while Kilian will dream
about the film of the future
and the cats will dream
their zen dreams
about nothing
like all the space in Chinese painting
allowing an image
to emerge

ALL IS BEAUTY

so when the lights go out
as they do and will
we are bereft of the whir
of all our devices
and the quiet envelopes us
like it did our ancestors
who never listened
to air conditioners
or refrigerators
something I have incorporated
and do not hear
consciously

I live in the woods
and trees are the giants
and they fill with frogs
and crickets and cicadas
who sing like
I breathe

so losing my lights
is a gift
I still have power enough
in the battery of my computer
to type though I hear every key
I compress
as well as the rhythm
of my breath

it may be minutes
or even hours
and if something big
has gone awry
maybe tomorrow

but for now
let my heartbeat
entrain
with beauty
and may I merge
with beauty
and may all things
be beauty

there is no me no we no I
all is echo and refrain
all is beauty

ACUPUNCTURE

I have been phobic about needles all my remembered life
when I was a child I had to be chased and captured
at the pediatrician's office before they could give me a shot
back then needles were reused after sterilization
and had to be sharpened and were often not

as an adult I advise anyone using a needle to inject me
or take blood that I will look the other way
and appreciate distracting conversation
rarely has it been painful
modern needles are sharp and disposable

I have had acupuncture in the past
but it was by a novice and neither helpful
or disturbing
over the past few years as I have grown into
my seventies
I have had some minor maladies
needling but not dangerous
perplexing because I could not find remedies

acupuncture with a pro is not cheap
and as in all the healing arts
there are those whose practice is exceptional
I knew of one
and when the light bulb came on in my head
why not try acupuncture
she put me on a waiting list

I declined a referral
I decided to wait
I was nervous about my first visit
this morning I met Faith
and we talked about needles

she told me in acupuncture school
they had to needle a balloon without bursting it
she said all the right things
and I stripped down to my skivvies
and got under the sheet on her table

she didn't do much
I think I counted 8 needles in my back
nothing more than a quick pinch
mostly barely noticed
left in for ten minutes
she told me to breathe
and left the room

she came back
and put in four more
in the part of my lower back
that has ached for weeks
put me under a heat lamp
with a temperature control in my hand
and left me for another ten
she finished with two quick pricks
in both of my hands
and I confirmed my next appointment

she said you will feel tired
and drink lots of water
I took two naps
my feet stopped tingling
my back has not hurt all day

I have energy to write
this thank you note to myself
at 11:15 in the evening

I think I'll send her
a copy in the morning

A Very Full Day

it rained for days before it stopped
and it's still hot
I noticed yesterday the zinnias in the pot
were wilting
the morning glory vines that haven't bloomed
drooping
and the floating fountain in the bird bath
that hadn't had enough sun to make a splash
was splashing
but the water in the bath
was evaporating

I spent more than an hour
back and front
to give my plants
a drink of water
I had to do this early
the heat was coming fast

I showered and went
for an overdue haircut
my stylist Stephen
is an elfin fellow
warm and talkative
as always, he does superlative work
his colleague at the desk
makes costume jewelry
I bought a "ruby" bracelet
as a birthday gift for tonight
I got home in time to make spinach pasta
and a shrimp and shitake
Vidalia onion and red pepper

My Ordinary Life

stir fry
I barely had time to eat it before
my first client and I
connected on Skype
would that it was not confidential
after we talked I cleaned the kitchen
put up the food
froze half of it
and took a nap
I gave myself 36 minutes
I had promised a long ago friend
in a faraway place a return call
and we talked
about his grief
how his husband died
as he gave him mouth to mouth
their eyes locked
until the last breath was taken
about how his cancer had come back
and another round of therapy was suggested
and how tired he was
we met when he was twenty and I was forty
and we cavorted all over Bali
he is in his fifties and I am in my seventies
and we talked about death
and I apologized for not having more time
and promised another call this weekend
I saw two more clients
both in duress for things outside of their control
I like them both a lot
and know that the range of emotions
they expressed were legit
would that I could say more

I was in a rush to collect myself
and get to the birthday party
it was not far away
and Google Maps
proposed a route
that involved seven turns
for an 8 minute journey
I followed my nose

when I arrived and parked
and was collecting the wine and rubies
an African American matriarch
appeared on her front porch
and asked me to back up my car
so as not to block her mailbox
I did, saying yes ma'am
I later learned she was indeed
the matriarch of her community

the party was hosted by my friend's
daughter and son-in-law
her husband was there
her grandchildren
and a few cherished friends
I felt honored to be included
Marion and I have been friends
for over half a century
we went to college together
and after college worked with disabled people
in rural South Georgia
she and second husband Mike have just moved to Decatur
my community, where her daughter and family also live

this was an intimate space
and confidentiality applies here too
but I can make general statements
like the food was delicious
I enjoyed the friends and family
some reminiscing occured that reminded me
of the long ago and far away
I felt so lucky
we are still here
we can still laugh and sigh
and share

and it fascinates me to see the play of genes
to meet her daughter
and see in her, her mother and her father
and well, let me stop short lest I say too much
except the youngsters, the grans
are also endowed with the loveliest genes

I left the party a little early
I just don't have the social stamina to play
I told my tired self as I drove the 8 minutes home
you've had a very full day
you've had a very full day

ANCIENT ART

I have friends from other eons
who look back at me
some dog faced
some bat winged
some bulging with child

I have friends from other eons
who have scribbled love notes
who have sealed their graves
with images of animals
who are lying still
in their own sarcophagus

they do not mumble or wink
when I visit
there is no visible movement
or sound my ear can hear

but I know below my senses
they know that I am here
and they are here
and their hello
is old as eons
in words no longer spoken

I cannot hear them
but I do

for my "friends" at Emory University's Carlos Museum

AND ON AND ON

so I hear about a friend in dire straits
organ failure, non responsive, talk of end of life
and I speak with our friends
who also love her
and we are all dismayed, disoriented
how could this be
when yesterday she was sending texts
her distress was real
she went from doctor to hospital
to icu and a ventilator
organ failure
how could we not weep
our friend is just past 60
she always cared more about us
than we cared about ourselves

when our hearts stop beating
we die
not before or after
we die
not because we wish
or we don't
I woke up my father
who had fallen asleep
despite his best efforts
his wife, my mother had expired
her face was the face
of peace

I don't know if my friend will make it
each of us has a time of departure
maybe she will wake and maybe
she won't

I know somewhere in the future
maybe years, maybe decades
I will be floating out to sea
and my friends will not be ready
they will pray I will come back
and if I could I would kiss them all
on the top of their heads
and whisper in their beloved ears
I love you

all is as it should be
we come when we come
and we go when we go
glory hallelujah

so dear friend
whether you go or stay
know that your love
will linger in my heart

listen, listen, listen
to my heart song
I will never forget you
I will never betray you

listen, listen, listen
to my heart song
you will always be with me
your love will linger on

and on and on

ANNIVERSARY

the anniversary of a death
is called a Yahrzeit in the Hebrew tradition
a candle is lit by a portrait of the departed
a prayer is said, a Kaddish is read
to place the departed with the ancestors
in the Celtic countries it is what is known
as a thin place
a place between the earthly and celestial
where messages might pass through

two years ago on this day
my mother passed away
it was peaceful she was home
in her own bed and ready to go
we were prepared for her death
got to say goodbyes
she lasted just long enough
for my father to survive

we had a small family gathering at her church
(this was the time of Covid,
though she did not die that way)
and another when her ashes were enniched
in the columbarium there
an obituary was published in Nashville
and another in Ft. Myers

and we went about our lives
taking care of her end of life business
making sure my father was cared for
sorting out her effects
reading old letters
things were not so surprising

no mysteries emerged
we each grieved privately
and tried to give each other solace

I don't remember anything usual
about last year's anniversary
don't remember what was said
no candle was lit
no message emerged

and now another year has passed
and I have had no call from family
and did not call them either
I told a few people
but there was little to say
my mother had stayed 91 years
and when she left
she wanted to go away

ANOTHER DAY

my Easter Uber driver
was Jesus
who drives part-time
and is taking a break
to visit his 84 year old mother
6 hours south of the border
with Mexico
Jesus takes me
from my father's home
to the Omni International
in downtown Nashville
I get there an hour early
and buy lemonade
and a muffin
blueberry my barista suggests
and wait at an outside table
watch the tourists on foot
and on scooter
one lady glides by
and I think my oh my
and crashes out of my eyesight

at exactly a quarter til liftoff
the door to my bus opens
I have the same driver
and the same steward
I had on my way up

Vonlane promotes first class transportation
this afternoon there are only four passengers
and our steward took a break
and our driver, who I praised

for his deft navigation the trip before
was resolved to get us back
in under four hours
I don't know his record
but he far surpassed mine

I slept through the boring parts
and watched as we went up and down
Monteagle Mountain
around Moccasin Bend
and maneuvered through a city
of steep embankments
and low retaining walls
no wonder I have been terrified
Chattanooga is as unsafe
as Bogota or Caracas

I spent a full week with my father
after whom I am named, junior
and we could be no more different
he is still in his home, 95
memory fails him, he has little strength
and is unable to control
everything below

his hardworking caregiver
had a week off with grandkids
and I filled in
cooked, washed
did laundry
provided an audience
for my father to tell his stories

he and I were not close
after I was 3
between birth until then
he took care of me
when my mother couldn't
I have a faint memory
of him taking me
to his parents
after my brother was born
and never coming back

I was a fairy child
and he was an engineer
and 70 years passed
and not until after my mother died
did we reconnect
he needs me now
like I needed him then
I make him a sandwich
put a cookie on his plate
we say I love you
and my heart knows
his heart means it

I am a lucky guy
it took seventy years
and we don't cry
I say goodbye Dad
and Jesus comes to take me away
in a blue Nissan
and what will be what
is assigned to another day

Barb Was Special

honestly I thought she was just uncommonly
pretty
when I saw her at professional events
she was always warm
we had friends in common
and when I decided to try my luck
at a second office in the suburbs
she was my muse

Barb had rented and renovated
a suburban house
and turned it into a psychotherapy palace
it was not to my taste
very country cosy
and the office I rented on Mondays
from her friend and colleague Pat Wells
was also not my style
thought I took many a long nap
on the craftsman framed
long black leather couch

so when I signed on to work there
I had an unusual series of meetings
with Barb, Pat and Nancy, the other tenant
we became very friendly with each other
and then Barb and Pat
invited me to become a part of a writing group
they were just beginning
and I couldn't say no
even though I wanted to

I thought I'll just hover for a few sessions
ten years later we were saying goodbye

I'm no good at math but it seems a decade has passed
and that Pat died in December and Barb died in February
in Covid times where there were no visits
no funerals

I have spoken with both of their spouses
taken and received food from our dear friend Emily
opened my heart and received blessings
from our friends LaDonna, Jill, Craig, Rae Lynne
and Roger

my mother died in August and three of my friends have lost
their mothers since
I spoke with Pat a week before she died
and we believed she was coming back to life
my mother, the minute she saw my tears
told me two things
death is okay and she was not dying yet

it took nine days
Pat died in hours
Barb in months

it is impossible to be born
before your birthday
or to go before
god opens the door

Barb lives on in my heart
and in Nick's heart, Gayle's heart
and in LaDonna's heart

she was, not to brag
our radiant friend
she just glowed
from the inside out

love had not come easy to Barb
she found it
in the diamond
of her heart

BECAUSE OF ART

I should have called an Uber
but decided to let Google Maps call the shots
and indeed she (the loud insistent female voice)
got me there to Parking Deck T
where I drove in circles for fifteen minutes
trying to find a spot

I found a spot
near the North Auburn Avenue elevator
which after photographing with my phone
I rode down a floor
and exited
looking for the tall building on Park Place
that I found willy nilly
and then elevated to the 23rd floor
and looked for the auditorium

it was a room with windows overlooking the city
named for a poor student who died in car crash
funded by his parents, his bust overlooking
hours and hours of education
out the back windows
the golden dome of the Georgia State Capitol

I met my hosts Renee and Dionne
and my dear friend Maurice
who had coaxed me into this talk
he was as always looking like a movie star
he introduced me
and I felt taller

earlier today I had a home health visit
from a no-nonsense nurse
who asked me to remember
apple, orange, banana
and to describe where the hands of the clock
would fall at 3:30
I passed the test
and when she asked me who was President
I said
"Biden, thank god."

the talk was hybrid
meaning there were people in the room
and people on Zoom
and the camera wasn't prepared
so I had to twist and turn

after I talked about how art
heals us and reveals us
and I read poems about AIDS
and Covid
and said what I often say
"depression is the repression
of expression"
and that art gives us hope
that we can overcome
as we always have
there is nothing
we have not overcome

I sat down
and the honorees of the competition
were featured
one young woman read her poem
about being locked down

an older woman showed her painting
of herself sick with Covid
a young woman
a work of art herself
showed her abstract painting
of a mix of emotion
another young woman
explained her video
of a friend who was murdered
during the pandemic

I had brought my picture book
of the National Memorial for Peace and Justice
in Montgomery to pass around
and just before I left
Maurice brought it back to me

I admit I was a little bit lost in leaving
the older woman whose painting of her illness
was so stunning rode down the elevator with me
I asked her if she had long Covid
and she said yes, she felt very ill
and that some days were better than others

I couldn't find the door I left from
but found another into the Parking Deck
and by some miracle of faith found my car
and drove home a different way
through neighborhoods
I have known for decades
their familiarity
a balm for my blister

I cannot talk about the AIDS years
without tears
I cannot separate those
fears from
Covid before vaccines
the visiting nurse asked me
if I had anxiety
and I said yes
she did not ask me why
the answer is obvious
it is a painting of a person
in pain
it is a film about a life interrupted
it is a poem about living
inside of fear

and it is a room overlooking the city
where friends can gather
speak truth to experience
and part being bigger and stronger
and better
because of art

BEYOND

I don't miss my mother much
she was not like a friend or a lover
I did not speak to her daily
or every week
we visited two times a year
and I sent flowers
for Mother's Day
and her birthday
just shy of Christmas

and yet we shared everything important
I knew the story of her life
and have inherited all of her costume jewelry
none of which I remember her wearing

she told me she was raised by a blue eyed
Black woman named Mattie
her mother worked as a stenographer
and her father a real estate attorney
she was pretty in her pictures
and was always in the shadow of her brother
two years older, handsome and smart
an athlete and valedictorian

she told me her father told her
to find a husband
he had grown tired of paying
for her education
and she was popular
petite and witty
and found my father
who was tall and handsome
and could fix things

she thought she couldn't get pregnant
told me different stories about why
an immature womb, a burst of fertility
after birth control failed
she said she had never held a baby
before I was born

she was in labor and anguish
for more than a day and night
until her lower body was numbed
by a saddle block
and I stuck my bloody head
out of her womb

she was in postpartum depression
until her hormones changed
three and a half years later when
my younger and only brother was born

in those first three years it was up to my father
and the pediatrician and my grandmothers, great
grandmother
great aunts and grandfathers to make sure I was happy
I enjoyed the competition
and could hold my breath until I turned blue
and fainted
to get attention

I wish I still had that skill

when my mother willed herself to die
last August
I got to bring her the morphine
that allowed her to finally relax
when I woke in the middle of the night

to bring her another dose
she was lying still as a stone
my father curled beside her
asleep in their mammoth bed

the light in the room was diffuse
the silence of the night was profuse
nothing moved, no breath
no pulse
I woke my father
said she is gone

my mother always very pretty
was in beautiful repose
the soft light in the room
had turned her into gold
and the peace on her face
all suffering gone
was the peace of god

she had gone beyond

BREATH BY BREATH

save me from my life
you ask
and I reply
I pause
I can't
I say
and sigh
you ask why

I remember
asking
and being told
we live between
heaven and hell
I remember being told
if there are angels
there are demons
of course there are

I have learned
and must learn
again and again
that the only life
I can save
is my own
and again and again
angels above me
demons below me
I save my life
breath by breath

all I can offer
breath by breath
is not a way to live
that is yours my friend
to figure out
but breath by breath
I live
I cannot die
until I do

breath by breath
breath by breath
breath by breath

BURNING BRIGHT

in every dream
I am on a journey
I just don't know where
I don't have a ticket
marked with a final destination
I am just going

when I wake up in the morning
odds are Ferdinand will be sleeping
by my feet and quite indifferent
to the light that fills the room
his sister Zephyr will come in
like the Town Crier and inform me
sun up open the door
open the window shades
and scratch her head

after a while
Ferdinand being my undertow
who says with his silky fur
why get up
stay here cuddled up
and Zephyr like an airline stewardess
preparing us for landing
says what are you waiting for
human
arise

and I always do
asking Ferdinand's indulgence
as I awkwardly slide my feet
from under the covers

and maybe he opens an eye
the message is why

when I do get up
and rub his head
I say I am so lucky
to have this day with him
and his sister
and I am

no matter what happens
or doesn't
we are nested warm
in our cozy corner
even when the night is cold
and the whistle of the train
blows blue

tomorrow will be the same bowl
of buttered grits
the same improvised sandwich
the takeaway dinner
and tomorrow night when
there is no light
and we hear the train whistle
in the dark
we are not disturbed

Ferdinand is sleeping
by the window sill
and Zephyr is sleeping
in her nook
in the bookshelf
and I am typing
tired and grateful

no hunger here
no fear of pirates
only the cold, cold night
and our fire burning bright

CAIRO

why wouldn't there be
miscommunication when shipping
half a ton of books (literally)
from Atlanta to Mumbai?

the FedEx driver who appeared on time
did not have a hand truck or a big truck
I showed her the boxes
and told her to call her supervisor
which she did
he and I talked later
and I told him these boxes
are really heavy
full of books
half a ton of books

he seemed to understand
but sent a truck yesterday
which I missed because
I was sitting in my sunny backyard
talking with a client
I had told the supervisor
not to send someone
until the day after

when I returned the call from FedEx
after an exhaustive series of prompts
I finally talked with a nice man
with a Spanish accent
and explained to him this dilemma

he told me they couldn't schedule a pick-up
more than two days in advance
and I didn't argue that today would be one day
and tomorrow two days

math is exact, alas
picking up deliveries
is more about myth
than math

so I got up early today
hoping for the best
and a little before noon
I heard the truck pull up

my Superhero FedEx guy
quickly surveyed the problem
and took the first box out
on his shoulder from the
furthest room
and then applied his strategy
to the other eleven boxes

each must have weighed a hundred pounds
18x18x16 and full of books
I held the door open twelve times
so the cats would not run under foot

he stacked them in front of my house
and then fetched his hand truck
he flattened it so he could take four boxes
on three trips
hefting each up on his truck

I asked if I could take his picture
and he agreed
I asked about his hair braided
in an elaborate beard under his chin
he said he got his first white hairs at eleven
and started losing his hair at seventeen
and learned to care for his hair
his eyes were amber
his body was lean and mean
though under his FedEx suit
nothing seemed extraordinary

I commended him on his strength
and offered a token of appreciation
the last question I asked him
what is your name
he said Cairo
and I asked him about the spelling
he said like the city

and then Cairo
and my half a ton of books
drove off in a FedEx truck
next stop Chicago
next stop Mumbai

Cairo took the cargo
on his shoulders
to his truck
next stop Chicago
next stop Mumbai

CAIS PIER

I could not imagine
as a child
a pier
longer than the one
my grandparents built
onto the Bon Secour River
I would sit on the end of it
far as I could be from land
and sing hymns
with my whole heart
never imagining
that anyone could hear me
I would sing about blood
and abandonment
and finding a gold ring
in the mud
I would sit and sing
and the sun would set
and my grandmother
would make supper
I could smell
and I picked up my feet
and walked the planks
rough with splinters
and opened the door
to the screened porch
and the next door
into the house
full of the aroma
of supper
and I forgot about
the pier

until it was tomorrow
when I would take
the hymnal
to its end
and sing
and sing
and sing
again about the 99 safe
and the one far away
and the golden ring of faith
and the power
the power
the power in the blood

Cais is Portuguese for pier.
Milton Nascimento also made it into a song.

CATCHING MY BREATH

it has been a swift rabbit
and I know it is playing a game of chase
if I dart this way
it darts that way
if I lunge it hops
if I freeze it bolts
if it freezes I sneak closer
and closer
and then faster than a sneeze
it is out of my reach

I have tried the mode of leisure
laying about with those lazy cats
wastes half the day
my Mamaw often woke my sleeping 13 year old
with the vacuum cleaner
and the song lazy bones
what you gonna do
how you gonna sleep the whole day through
sleepin in the noonday sun

I would get up and eat my cereal
and then follow her in her gardening chores
even stomping on huge grasshoppers
before we had Vienna sausage sandwiches
on white bread with mayonnaise
and thinly sliced sweet gherkin pickles

we would sit on the screen porch
with the oscillating fan
and drink ice tea
and listen the the symphony
of the birds

I think I got to read in the heat
of the afternoon
and when Papaw came home
look at his collections of stamps and coins
he would often have a bag of stamps for me
clipped off envelopes from the huge real estate office
he ran downtown
I would carefully soak them off their envelopes
and arrange them in the stamp books he gave me
and I would sort pennies and nickels and dimes
and put them in round slots in the coin books he gave me

after supper
and maybe a little black and white television
he would ask who would like a little bit of ice cream
and my grandmother and I would chime in
we would
I declined the offer of ice cream and jello
I just wanted ice cream most often vanilla
with a windmill cookie
just what you need for sweet dreams
on gentle breezes

I would wake up the next morning
later than I should and hear
the hum of the vacuum cleaner cleaning
and the plaintive voice of my Mamaw

lazy bones
what you gonna do
how you gonna sleep the whole day through
sleepin in the light of the sun

my cats don't run the vacuum
or have a song to rouse me
they are snuggled in and sleep
beside my thigh
or between my feet
and on cloudy days
when the sun hides behind the haze

their lazy bones
join mine
resting for a little more time
sleeping off the grief
another few minutes
and another few minutes
and another half hour
of relief

CLOUD

I was born with big ears
and so I listen
I listen in person
I listen on the phone
I listen with a webcam
on the Internet

my three clients
all virtual
told me Covid stories
one was just waiting
his family and friends
all fallen down
one had Covid
ten days of headaches
and lethargy
I made him laugh, cry
and the pink was in his cheeks
before we said goodbye
the third had lost his father
to Covid and spent ten days
of grief alone in his room
after he had tested positive
for the virus

this made it hard for me
to shake my feet
and waiting for the new employee
to process my simple Western Union
made me want to holler at her boss
train your people!
I did not, I saw him driving a buggy
back to his store from the parking lot

and teased him
"you are having too much fun"

when I got my groceries organized
I took my solid nap
the one I tell myself I don't need
and after 30 minutes
I begin to slowly come back

I don't "need" a nap
I hear my father in my head
and if I reply
mutuality is lost on him
"Dad, we need a nap."

the help you pay for
is not just for you
but for your descendants
who do not wish our grief
to be burdened with worry

our mother worried for you both
and when she left us
we worried for your heart
her soul
our own renewal

day after day
and night after night
you find repose
and alight with the light
you make your bowl
of cereal
and brew your coffee
and when the housekeeper arrives
and makes your lunch

you sit with her at the table
and eat

after she feeds you dinner
and in the dark of the evening
leaves
you play your music
close the blinds
and in time
find your bed and sleep

in the elbow of the night
we are all sleeping
we are on an island
sometimes pacific
sometimes terrific

you wake up
from your King Lear dreams
and life is more treacherous
than it seemed
and when you begin
to inflate reality
with the impossible
and I say no, stop
I can't agree

you fall back
into uncertainty
and I look up
at a mountain
whose peak
is in a cloud

Cold Cucumber Soup

my friend Bill told me
he had an overabundance
of cucumbers in his garden
big ones, organic
green and knotty
I gave one away
served one in salad
and still had three
I did not want to pickle

it has been a number of years
since I made a cold soup
I know the recipe by heart
cucumbers peeled and seeded
a small slice of sweet onion
a couple of sprigs of fresh dill
in a blender or food processor
combined with, my favorite
whole milk yoghurt
now you could substitute
coconut milk
sour cream
or half and half
(add a little lemon juice for tang)
but the fresh dill is essential
salt to taste

it is one of those things
that takes less time to make
than clean up from
and the results
are best the next day

cold, cold
and sip by sip
penetrating palate
and gut
pushing up a smile
an ahh
a summer song

cucumber, cucumber
make me a soup

CREME BRULEE

I lost my creme brulee virginity in Paris
in a little restaurant in the Marais
where ruby slippers decorated our alcove
I don't remember the entree
but we drank good wine
we six me and Neil and Raven
Ilene and Linda and Kareem

Kareem was from Morocco
Neil had hooked up with him
outside the the gay bar Le Quetzal
when it closed for the night
I didn't know he was a hustler

this got us thrown out of our cozy hotel
and we found another just a block away
none of us spoke French except Kareem
who got us into the fast track to the Louvre
and into this jewel box where after much wine
creme brulee
creme brulee
came to our table
and Kareem showed us how
to crack the glaze with a fork
and we oohed and aahed
and I have never forgotten

tonight
with old friends Nancy and Pauline
at Babette's Cafe
after entrees and wine
we had creme brulee

my first since Covid lockdown
I cracked the glaze
and ate the custard
and oohed and aahed
in homage to Kareem

Continuing Education

I am a licensed healthcare professional
who is required to purchase continuing education
at least 25 live, "synchronous" hours
with 10 more thrown in for non-synchronous study
every two years to renew my license

I finished my requirement today
with six hours detailing how Intimate Family Systems Theory
and Polyvagal Theory are interconnected and interwoven
the phrase "old wine in new skins" occurred to me more
than once
but I have no complaint
I got my final 6 hours
and the presenter was fluent in these languages

Intimate Family Systems
is a 3.0 to the 2.0
Transactional Analysis
derived from the 1.0
a la Freud
superego, ego and id
it's all about the parts
inside us

Polyvagal Theory reveals
the not so astounding fact
that our nervous systems
are primal and reactive
especially around survival
fight, flight and freeze
something Darwin noticed

and before Freud and Darwin
were philosophers and physicians
dating back to the dawn of civilization
these are primal postures and questions
how do we survive
and how do we mend from trauma

I was in vaccine fatigue today
and grief
and worn out by a week of too much
death and dying
and physical maintenance
and after I finished my synchronous
seminar during which I ironed shirts
made the bed
cleaned the cat boxes
and comforted friends whose grief
was deeper than mine
I took a little nap
and sighed and sighed again
to right my nervous system

I had dinner with a friend
who was almost as tired as me
but showed up
before I faded
and took me to a familiar place
with familiar food
for dinner

Athens Pizza
is an old Atlanta restaurant
Greek food is the specialty
and Kilian got the gyro
and I got more eggplant parmesan

than I can eat at three sittings
our waiter was a curious fellow
very polite and engaging
and when it was time to pack the food
and pay the bill
I said to him
your accent is unfamiliar
and he asked me to guess
where he was from
and hinted it was near Greece
Bulgaria, I said
nice try said he
I am from a country where you can swim to Greece
not Albania I thought
Turkey? and he said yes, his village was near Izmir
on the blue Mediterranean and he could swim to Greece
he said lots of Africans took that route

he was a cute guy with a crop of dyed blond hair
and who knows how many tattoos
once he opened up he said he had been roaming
  the world
getting a tattoo in every country
and said the black bands around his arm
were for his ex-lovers
he said he had left one tattoo uncovered
hoping that ex might come back
he said he is a perpetual student
almost in reach of a PhD in clinical psychology
he said he hoped we would come back

Kilian came in for tea and cats
and we talked about where consciousness comes from
and I speculated we needed it since we were such poor
hunters

he said we were the nerds of all species
and we talked about how hermit crabs navigate
versus cats versus us
and I mentioned maybe mushroom spores
from a cosmic collision
might have turned the light switch on
how we need community
more than our primate cousins
and had to learn to name each other
and speculate about the future
and then I succumbed to vaccination fatigue
or just a long day
my polyvagal system
in need of a reboot
my parts all in agreement

wind down dear one
listen to the froggie
lullaby
outside your window
feel your shoulders slump
wrap yourself in the shroud
of your grief
and hum yourself
 to sleep

Conversation With The World

Nuumo said to his bewildered son
"comfort him"
Chris, the oldest of ten, was barely nineteen
and in his culture he was still treated as a child
I was his father's American brother
come to celebrate his 50th birthday
I had special clothes for the occasion
as did Nuumo and his wife Princess
and all ten children
and I entered with my friend
shoulder to shoulder
my friend the high priest of the Ga
the million plus people
who live on the coast of Ghana
and in Accra its capital

I had been with Nuumo
when the cow was selected
and I had been instructed/intimidated
by his henchman Da
to be present
when the cow was murdered
it was brutal
I watched from a distance
there was no mercy
for the animal
and no revelry from us
the observers
we watched quietly as Da
took the animal down

with blows from a hammer
and scorched its hide with a torch
and began dismemberment
no one whispered
no one cried
no one held out a hand to be held

I could leave once the butchery commenced
I had no inkling of what would come
hours later I put on the white clothing
of the royal family
and walked into the celebration
amid cheers and applause

my head was spinning
I had a hard time catching my breath
my costume made of shiny polyester
felt like a trap
I was nauseous
I whispered in Nuumo's ear
I am getting sick
he ordered a bicarbonate of soda
it didn't work
I knew I would faint
I told him I had to go
I know it would be odd
not a good omen
but getting sick
in front of all his guests
chiefs and priests and the King of the Ga
would be worse

that is when he told his eldest son
to escort me back to my room
my special room, just for me

in his newly built stone and marble palace
I stripped off my polyester suit
streaming sweat and cold as ice
Chris piled my clothes on top me
as I shivered
and sank into my bed
I looked at him
and he looked at me
he was terrified

I had been sick this way before
maybe it was food
or just a virus I had never encountered
Nuumo called a doctor
who came and examined me
he was concerned
but there was nothing to do
I was weak, I was trembling
but the fever and chills were subsiding
and I, just short of delirium
was in and out of sleep
I could hear the celebration
reverberating through my open window
and it seemed like an endless hallucination
was I dreaming
the drums were beating
and for a few hours the dawn was quiet
until the drums were beating again
and the revelers were dancing and drinking
the rest of the liquor
and eating the last of the cow

and I slept and woke in the afternoon
I bathed and dressed
and walked slowly up the hill

to the place where I sat under a tree
where the breeze was gentle
and cooling
and slowly I came back to life
and one by one the children
came to look at me
Princess asked one of their helpers
to climb the coconut tree
and toss down a coconut
and open it with a machete
and I drank the water
and ate the meat
and was once again
in conversation
with the world

DAL

I didn't taste dal
until I was almost thirty
and I didn't know what
I was tasting

dal is not lentils
but the love of lentils

there are a million recipes
by a million grandmothers
each with a different chemistry
more than lentils
and water

onions and salt
and spice are essential
butter makes everything
better

I like tomatoes
garlic and ginger
lemon juice
but not too much
cumin and mustard seeds
fennel and fenugreek
roasted and crushed
and when I am cooking
for friends who like heat
peppers

dal goes with rice
dal goes with curry
dal needs a little raita

and a tiny bite of pickle
and it is extra nice
to have tandoori bread
or puri
to scoop the dal

I cannot scoop
and bring everything
neatly to eat
I cannot scoop
without dripping

a friend once excused me
she said we have done this
since childhood and I smiled back
and asked for more dal
and more bread

DEEPER DINNER

I belong to a dinner group
8 of us older gay men
tonight with Marvin missing
at 71 I am the youngest

every now and then
we plan a field trip
and today we visited
Atlanta's Jewish museum
the Breman

we passed through extra layers
of security
and one of our member's sister
a volunteer docent took us on a tour

the first exhibition was a revelation
Jews were less than one percent
of pre Nazi Germany
only a few had wealth
and yet their demonization
drove the rise of Hitler

in less than a year
the Nazis went from fringe party
to dictatorship
in less than a year
all political opponents
were imprisoned
all media was controlled
and all Jews were targeted

over the whole of Nazi Europe
there were more than ten thousand camps
in easy view as were the mass graves
everyone knew

and there were a few
who sheltered
a few who gave passage
a few who risked everything
so a few Jews could survive

the second exhibit was about
the history of chutzpah
in Georgia and Alabama
how Jews were an integral part
of their communities
and both vilified and honored
from Leo Frank to Senator Ossoff
our friend whose sister was our docent
called us all to pause
as a video of their father
Gus Sr.
told part of the story

we had an hour before dinner
and walked a circuit on Atlanta's beltline
saw a red shouldered hawk
and made a wary passage
(there were active golfers)
around a golf course

we chose the fanciest Thai restaurant
in town to have our dinner
everyone said it was good

and all of us were titillated
dining with the glitterati

on my way back and forth to the restroom
(the urinals were filled with ice
to deter odor)
I saw lots of lobster shells
none of us had lobster
and we waited a long time for our birthday desserts
three of us with December birthdays
and complimentary lychee sorbet

I believe we all left in good humor
having balanced horror with delight
having embodied resilience
no matter the challenges of aging
no matter the woes of the world
no matter the wait or the price or the taste
we are here
we are here
we are here

"Deputy Robinson"

Deputy Robinson left me a message yesterday morning
I knew his call was coming since he obtained my number
from my professional listing on the Psychology Today site
and they always give a heads up email
he said he was calling from the DeKalb Sheriff's Office
he said it was about a warrant or citation
and it was imperative that I return his call
to a different number
extension 4 he said
when I called that number a recorded female voice
told me to call 911 if it was an emergency
and to listen closely as the options on their menu had
changed
there were many including extension 4
for Deputy Robinson
he did not answer
or answer from the number he called from
he did return my call and repeated in a message
how important it was that I call him back

I thought something was funny when
the voice on the recording
said Sheriff's office and did not mention which sheriff
I checked the numbers of the DeKalb County Sheriff
and none matched up with the numbers
Deputy Robinson had left on my voicemail

it was after hours and I decided that I would let it go
until morning
but I could not let go of my imagination
what had I done wrong?
or been wrongly accused of

had a neighbor complained
was a hair out of place
did I have a secret enemy
had I forgotten to pay a fine
for something I had couldn't recollect?

the worms crawl in
the worms crawl out
the worms play pinochle
on your snout

I waited until after breakfast
and called the number again
got the voicemail
I called again pressing 1 for extension 1
and 2 for extension 2
but they all took me back to . . . extension 4
and Deputy Robinson

I sent an email to the address listed for complaints
on the DeKalb County Sheriff's website
and got a quick reply from Captain Shields
she said I had been likely scammed
and left a number for me to call

she and I had a delightful conversation
evidently Deputy Robinson or whoever he is
is a frequent flyer
she said she received such calls herself
and after blessing out the caller
had her number blocked
she said don't answer
and certainly don't give money

strangely Deputy Robinson
has not called back

DRAG

means to pull
I used to have a dog named Blues
when we would go for walks
she would drag me
as we left the apartment
and I would drag her
as I brought her home

if drag were a contest
it is about resistance
it is about reverse magnetism
it is about slowing things down
it is about hesitating gravity

one of the honorifics of drag
is the title of queen
although there are also kings
but the queens have ruled
for millennia
drag is essentially a matriarchy

the queens deceive
with quickness, cleverness, a fast banter
and yet are pulling us back
a force of retrograde
blurring the lines
of what is fake
and what is real

retrograde is fake
the planets only seem to move
backwards

the naked eye
often misperceives the truth

drag in racing
is overcoming the inertia
of the swerving track
drag in ballrooms
is overcoming
the need to reconcile
gender and motion

move slowly
even if the music is fast
pulling you back
even as you dance
forward for dollars
your charm
is in seeming
to be above
the applause
your grace
is the grace
of rising
from
a fall

an homage to the drag queens
of the Boybutante Ball
Athens, Georgia 4/23/22

DELICIOUS

my friend Bob
made a chicken dish
with preserved lemon
that was inspirational
I will share the recipe
if you like

cooking is one of my rituals
something I do for body and soul
something I share for healing
and pleasure
even a vegetarian might enjoy
this recipe
substituting breadfruit
or tofu or paneer

it is all about spice
and heat and oil
and onions and garlic
it is all about sear
and steam in broth
or wine

and it is all about time
how much
at what temperature
and so life
is a recipe
isn't it

it sears us
and steams us
and holds us
in its sauce
and bubbles

time is the rice
we pour the sauce upon
it rises first to our nose
and then to our lips
and then bite by bite
and sip by sip
life has coaxed us
to live another day
by being delicious

Dinner Party

I never accurately estimate
how much movement
is requisite for me to cook
and serve guests
one is easy
two is fine
more than two
requires effort
which was nothing twenty years ago
but now past seventy
every movement is a calorie
it would be amusing
to count

I have an easy repertoire
I recommend a baking sheet
and a rice cooker
olive oil and rice vinegar
watercress if you can find it
sprouts and cucumbers
and a saute of vegetables
I cook salmon and chicken
and rarely pork
I try to time it for 45 minutes
after my guests arrive
for wine and cheese
or sparkling water
and roasted nuts

if it is just me and a pal
I may make quiche
or chili or vegetable soup

and cornbread
or pasta with a light sauce
or a rich sauce

I can season with curry
or Herbs de Provence
or Bengali seeds
butter or olive oil
or mustard oil
or coconut oil

I can vary the starch
rice or quinoa or farro
potatoes or naan
rice plus protein
maybe dal
and vegetables
and maybe a sweet
now and then

we sit at the table
and like every story in history
begin
maybe a prayer is mumbled
but all the same we are humbled
food from hearth to plate
food from plate to mouth
on cellular level we appreciate

we begin
our life again
one bite and then another
we begin

FEAR

it begins as a little shadow
something that scampers across
consciousness
it is reflected in surfaces
has a tiny echo
and then hides
until almost forgotten
it reappears as a noise
that is unfamiliar
you look around
and try to find it
it is not there

it returns once you forget it
puts its hand upon your shoulder
gives a shove
or pokes its finger in your side
and you shrug
who is it but by then
it disappears

you sleep a little ruffled
and your sleep takes you down
to that path by the river
where the moon is shining brightly
and you listen to the river
and the song it sings
and the night seems almost gentle
then you feel it on your neck
foul breath in your nostrils
foreboding but faceless

when you move
it seems to follow
you move faster
and then don't know
where you are
confused
you are
either running or frozen
and it is catching up
you hear the clatter
of hooves
you see the steam
of something breathing
oh my god you say
it will capture me
and just as it clutches
your shoulder or your hand
you wake up
make a sound
that is between a gasp
and a cry
turn on a light
look around the room
shiver
the snake did not bite you
but it tried

FINAL

I received a message
from my right knee
an SOS of sorts
I am not happy
so I applied the liniment
rested with pillows
and heating pad
a cat snuggled up
to my left calf
I tried to rest
and when I couldn't
picked up my cell phone
and made my Sunday call
to my father, 94
who lamented
he couldn't get to the bathroom
with enough dispatch
to avoid an accident
three in one night
he explained
he had to clean himself up
dress again
and wait for the next catastrophe
I am a fountain of empathy
but have run out of suggestions
he says this is how it is
and I say in sympathy
I am sorry
he says what else can you say
and wonders if he will live
a thousand more days
and I say, Dad

when the bus pulls up
get on the bus
and he says . . .

we repeat I love you
I hear this more from him
in the last few years
than in the first seventy years of my life
he says I am old
and I say Dad, I am old too
and he remembers
it is true
and I say, I hope tonight is better
and he knows that is love
and says it will be what it will be
and I say goodbye
and feel like I might cry
but I don't
at least for now
I hope
he can sleep without incident
and I can sigh

every time we speak
there is a note of farewell
every time we greet
there is I love you
every time we say goodbye
I know it might be final

he is final
I am final
we are final

FIVE OF DIAMONDS

it was completely saturated
on the asphalt in the parking lot
but I picked it up
I have a fascination for random cards
and so I put it first on the store circular
to dry it
and when I got into the checkout lane
I stuck it in a mandolin I was purchasing
the checkout clerk saw it lodged there
and thought it was debris
and took it out, tossed it aside

the five of diamonds is not a good card
it predicts insecurity, despair, isolation
I knew none of this
and I wanted to reclaim it
but I thought the cashier
would not understand
he thought it was litter

now that I know
I know it wasn't my card
maybe for a minute
but I did not have to take it
home

FLOAT

hardware

I needed an extra key for my garden gate
and I thought how many years have my toilet seats
served their purpose?
I bought new ones
I needed potting soil
but could not resist
buying mouse ear hostas
and a plant my Mamaw
brought back from the Smokies
Hearts-A-Bustin'

I had been to my guru/chiropractor
who pieces me back together
every few weeks
we talk about cats
and he moves my bones
tells me I am in alignment
so much so
I eat Chinese food for lunch
today I had the hot and sour soup

I did not buy candy
at the hardware store
sometimes I do
I like the old fashioned
Necco Wafers
but only the orange, pink, white
purple and yellow

I took pictures of flowers
in my garden
before I joined my poet friend Don
for dinner at Rain
they pour strong martinis
and make good sushi
and we talked about the essential
and the ethereal

on the way back home
the light came on
and tomorrow I will fill my tank
with gasoline
liquid gold

home, I feed the cats
settle back
distract my body
as my brain
distills the day
and that is that

I put CBD
on my aching knee
I click on comics
that amuse me
I know that sleep
is just around the bend
in the river
and the river
is just what time
looks like
in liquid form
and I know to float
is metaphorical

I could be a scoop
of ice cream
in root beer
or a blossom
from the top of my tulip tree
floating free
chevron of orange in yellow
in green
blessing my roof
and the ground that surrounds
and blessing me

FOG

the crest of a hill
birds in shadow
flying through
everything
disappearing

I can only see myself
if I wipe the steam
from the mirror
and for those seconds
the steam doesn't rise
I can see my eyes
seeing me

FOR RON LAMBE

who has heard a voice
who has had a calling
who could hear prophecy
in a waterfall

the wind has a voice
the water lapping on stones
the heat of the sun penetrating forests
the moon of soul breathing into soul

who has heard a voice
who has had a calling
who could hear prophecy
in a waterfall

For the Soft Ride Home

a banner in front of the Golden Buddha
INSIDE DINING OPEN WE MISS YOU
Chinese food comforts me
and I want Sizzling Rice Soup
that sounds like Rice Krispies
when the hot rice
hits the salty soup
I want Mongolian Beef
never good as takeaway
and my friend wants noodles
and asks me with what
shrimp I say
I want Shrimp Lo Mein
so our masked waiter
brings us our soup
and the rice sizzles
and we all exclaim in glee
then the sweet and salty beef
and green onions on crispy rice noodles
and the shrimp peeking through
the mound of lo mein
and we eat and sigh and eat and sigh

the tables are distanced
no one sits beside or behind us
I even eat my fortune cookie
with its silly message and numbers for the lottery

I don't want the leftovers
take them to your brother
I am sated
it was like a dream
from before the war
when it was safe to drive
for comfort food
and eat in peace
no rush
just one bite of this
and one bite of that
and enough left over
to perfume the car
for the soft ride
home

FOREVER #1

Lincoln's got his back
he is looking over the Tidal Basin
at Jefferson
and in the slant of the afternoon light
giving shade

he was a small man
and has a big statue
if you stand before him
he rises above you
I watched as people
posed for photographs
he was always a tower
no matter his stature
his arms folded
a scroll in one hand
he is not blinking
Jefferson cannot avoid
his gaze
no longer enslaved
his eloquence will echo
forever

at the Martin Luther King Memorial in Washington DC

My Ordinary Life

FOREVER #2

we began at the top
and it was fun
Little Richard's sequined coat
Chuck Berry's cadillac
Charlie Parker's saxophone
we descended through history
down from Civil Rights
to Jim Crow
and in the belly of the beast
Slavery
pushed a few steps further
we saw the persistence
of intolerance and struggle
Treyvon Martin's grey hoodie
with a bullethole in the chest
the Skittles, the tennis shoes, the iced tea
left us breathless
a kind docent
silver-haired and tall and handsome
asked us as we gasped for air
have you seen the fountain
and directed us
into a room of water falling
from a ring around the ceiling
quotations from Nelson Mandela
and Sam Cook etched on the walls
and nothing but the sound
of falling water
neither rain nor tears
but how water falls
and how water will fall
forever

at the National Museum of
African American History and Culture in Washington DC

FOREVER #3

I counted my steps
the first set then a terrace
then a second set
Dr. King's words inscribed
"I have a Dream"
and I arrived
it was cool
the sun was hot
but in this cavern of marble
it was cool
Lincoln was a giant
his words etched in stone
the sign asking silence
ignored
in many languages
I wanted a picture
Lincoln would not smile
but two little Black girls
cuter than cute
were smiling at their parents
in twenty years
I hope they are smiling at each other
and remember meeting Lincoln
a giant in a marble cavern
looking out at Washington
and the world he changed
forever

at the Lincoln Memorial in Washington DC

Fright

my father is shouting outside my bedroom door
"I heard the doorbell ring. Let's get the guns."
Cortisol rushes through my body.
This is the sixth night of seven.
He has slept through all the others.
I did not hear the doorbell ring.
(it rings loud and long 'My Country Tis of Thee Sweet
Land of Liberty')
I help him secure the parameters. All the doors are locked.
The porch light on.
He has both of his rifles and tells me the ammo is in
his bedroom.
I tell him I think we are okay. He lives in a condo
community full of street lights
and so quiet a neighbor could hear a pin drop.
I go back to bed and yet I see his light is on all night long.
He is guarding us from the interloper from his dreams.
My brother later tells me he has removed all the ammo.
I didn't know so I didn't go outside my room that night,
slept tight.

what a tragic headline, "Father Shoots Son in
Mistaken Identity"
my body full of stress hormones
dreams a dream about a house full of guests
and housemates far younger than me
and hallways waist deep in dust
and all the young ones drunk and rude
I wake myself up
take a pee
and know this is not my reality
and sigh that my father now ninety-three
cannot know in the deep of the night
when a dream only brings him a fright

French Fries

I tasted my first institutional french fries today
and had a little hamburger with mayo and pickles
and a Coca-Cola out of a machine
and sat out in the sun and consumed
as much as I could
and collected my debris
and took it back inside the store
as the outside trash can was at capacity

I had found a spot where I could eat in the shade
and when this older African American woman
(probably no older than me but with a cane)
came out with her brown bag
of a burger and fries
I was almost finished
wanted to signal her over
but before I could another patron
an older white man
(was he older than me?)
left his table
and so she moved into the shade
and I hope she enjoyed
her lunch

I paid almost $15 dollars for mine
and it was fine
but not worth $15
for a coke, some fries
and a burger on a bun with pickles

I patted myself on the back
I had waited more than a year
to sit and wait for ten minutes
on something so mediocre
that had risen in my imagination
high enough to have a halo   .

I tossed the halo with the leftovers
into the inside trash can
and drove on to my next destination
satisfied, ratified and not an ounce of regret

FRIED SHRIMP AND WAFFLES

I hadn't had in more than a year
a dozen plus a salad with blue cheese dressing
and a buttery baked potato
and a vodka martini straight up with a twist

my friend Kevin treated me
at our old haunt
Atlanta's Colonnade
frying shrimp and chicken
serving collard greens and cornbread
since 1927

my place to go for a treat
we teased each other in the parking lot
for the last year we have been walking
instead of dining
and promised to alternate the two

I almost inhaled the shrimp
dipped them into cocktail sauce
and tartar sauce
and told my friend
and this is true
I hadn't had as many calories
at a single meal
since before the madness

thanks to Moderna
I can hug my friends again
thanks to Pfizer
(and Doctor Fauci)

I can remove my mask
when I eat in public

I had breakfast in an outside garden
unmasked with my friend Cary
who works in Burundi
and when last we dined
it was before the time
when we sheltered in fear

he has a smile
that tames lions
and we look into each other's eyes
in wonder
we have now survived two plagues
and can gossip and reminisce
and eat waffles and eggs benedict

GARDENING

mountain mint
and elderberries
Rupert told me they were barriers
against invasives
something every gardener
has to consider

my garden has been doused
for almost a dozen days
the leaves are greener
and the blossoms fewer
so far no branch has fallen
and I am not holding my breath

my fraternity of trees
my sorority of birds
my complexity of branch
and flight and frog song
make a canopy
for me and the cats
and squirrels

we are on higher ground
not worried about floods
the frogs seemed bolstered
and tonight's concert
will be more aria
than ballad

and the cats and I will sleep
they on their porch
and me on my little bed

and the squirrels in their nests
and tomorrow will wake us up
as always
even though the sun makes no noise
when she cracks the dawn
like an egg

GENEROSITY

I remember being born
and it was not easy
there were no classes for pregnant couples
in 1950
it was supposed to be natural
my mother told me she threw up
when she found out she was pregnant
and the gestation period
was difficult
she was just 22
and I was her first child
she told me that she was in labor
for hours before she got a saddle block
that numbed her
and still it took a long time
for my tiny head
to crown
and she was so exhausted
from the labor
it was days before
she had the strength to hold me
and her milk ran dry
maybe this accounts for
my love of creamy things
maybe this accounts for
my fear of neckties

it was just luck
I was not born into a war zone
I was born with capable and doting
grandmothers and great aunts
that could pass me back and forth

and love me into life
no bombs were falling
no food shortages
oh no, there was always cake
and glasses of milk
and plates full of vegetables
and seafood
and cantaloupes
and watermelons
I still seek out these elixirs

my mother recovered from postpartum depression
after my brother was born
three and a half years later
her hormones rebalanced and this terrified
young woman got back her good mind
and her capacity to nurture

our family
was far from perfect
and there are stories
and stories for another time
but for this story
the baby whose passage
was long and strenuous
and whose early life
was was a game of toss
and who got more love
was held heart to heart
and never abandoned
never hungry
never terrified by bombs bursting
or marauders breaking down doors
it wasn't perfect
it never is

if I could have a dream come true
what was real
for me would be real for you
it wasn't perfect
but I was never afraid
and I will always
have more love
than I need
and know
that by generosity
I was delivered
and sustained
and live to give

GOLDEN AND COMPLETE

to say I fell asleep

is not accurate
I slept but in suspense
how many days and nights
did my mother linger
in the half light
of life and death

I learned how to draw
the blue fluid from the vial
to squirt in her cheek
she always wanted more

I learned to sit and be
as one must sit and be
when a loved one
is dying
in slow motion

we asked the nurses
how long, how long
and they said
soon, soon
but could not chart the hour

I was not sleeping
but listening
I knew I would
come to
I would go to the kitchen
open the fridge

and pull more blue liquid
into the syringe

only this time
this time
when I entered the room
my father curled in sleep
on the other side of the bed
my mother golden in diffuse light
and dead

the blue, blue morphine
no longer needed
I called my brother
she is gone
she is gone

something in my heart
unlocked
something that was holding on
I woke my father
told him she was perfect
and she was
golden and complete

HE DID NOT FALL

I felt like I was holding something fragile
precious, liquid, flammable
each step had to be deliberate
each toe in place
the arch and energy of each foot
aligned with bone and tendon
the sway of my hips
the point of balance
three fingers below the navel
all pivot perfect

I had on white gloves
not real ones but my hands were clean
and my fingers nimble
as I sorted through old photographs
little cards from a wedding long past
a yellowed will and an old death certificate
when all were sorted into saved
and unsaved
my father who was standing above
looking down, hands clutching his walker
grew tearful
catching each breath
a net for his tears
he said he hadn't been ready to say farewell
this time last year when my mother died
Nancy, my brother's wife
said we all miss Mimi
my brother told him it was okay
and I held this fragile swan
made of air and fire and water
it did not shatter

every night of my visit
I slept in the bed my mother died in
on the side of the bed where she lay
where she breathed her last breath
I could hear my father up and down all night
he can't evacuate his bladder
he can't ever have rest
I hear the flush and again the flush

in the morning I am up
and he is reading the paper
drinking his coffee
doing sudoku
and I am far from rested
alert to his breath
and movements

it is as if I can't divert attention
lest he slip
I can only use half of me
lest he fall

I make it through my tour of duty
careful to a tremble
and when I pack the car
and tell him I love him
I mean it
he echoes back
and stands to watch me leave

hours later, after I call him
and tell him I have driven
the five hours from Nashville
to Atlanta
he falls

My Ordinary Life

he hurts himself
tears flesh
but does not break bone
my brother comes and takes him
for emergency care
texts me pictures of his wounds

this morning I call my father
he answers, says yes he fell
one foot went back before it should
and that he is ok
if there was a God I believed in
I would pray O Heavenly Father . . .

destiny is anything that happened
ten minutes ago
anything that happened ten minutes ago
is God's will

I don't know what God will do
or what he/she/they won't
but I know for ten days
I balanced fate in my hands
I did not falter
I did not stumble
I did not drop
he did not fall

Hello, Hello, Hello

the voice on my GPS was accurate
she told me where and when to turn
and I followed her instructions
and after 11 prompts
found my destination

yellow irises were blooming in profusion
in the circular driveway
in front of my friends' house
I arrived simultaneously with my friend Rupert
our friend Dan V met us at the door
of the home of Waqas and Maryam
and although it is Ramadan
and Maryam is devout
we still had tea and samosas
and cheese and kabobs
and crackers and cookies
and more tea

Waqas writes with his nose
and reads us a memoir full of scents
the smell of rain and roses
Dan V writes with his memory
of being a boy and building a boat
and being a boy and feeling remote
and Rupert drives us down a ditch
where our wheels dig out a trench
for frogs to breed
and succeed
I read about waking up from trauma
confused, where are my bandages
where are my bandages?

GPS gets me back on the road home
and I am more relieved than annoyed
at the commands to turn and turn and turn
I throw it all off and go rogue
when I stop at Kroger's

I buy potato chips
for my friend Dan G's birthday
and guilty treats
Cheetos and Fritos
for my trip to Nashville

tomorrow will be full of storms
and Sunday full of sun
so Sunday morning
me and my bags of crunch
will start early

tomorrow the rains
will water the garden
I will pack my bags
for an early departure
I filled the tank, got a 3% discount on gasoline

I will arrive midday in Nashville
time for lunch and time for dinner
I will catch up with my ninety-three year old father
who remembers off and on I am coming
we will be glad again and again
for another hello, hello, hello

HIGH SCHOOL MEMORY

I signed up for a program
to befriend a disabled person
I was assigned to Robbie
and he was assigned to me
we met several times
over the course of months
Robbie was older than me
he had cerebral palsy
and might have been very handsome
had his face not been contorted
his speech was contorted too
he spoke slowly and without articulation
I had to lean in close
to listen about his job at the slaughterhouse
when the cow was brought before him
it was his job to shoot the cow in the head
he did this every day
time after time
he shot the cow in the head
so I could have hamburgers

I did not connect the dots
after a while there was nothing left to say
I went on to college
and Robbie held one shaking hand
with the other
and did his best
to kill the cows he shot

HOVER OR FLEE

I have a line that is sometimes a circle
sometimes a box
I draw it with chalk
sketch it with charcoal
rake it with leaves and pine straw

I have rules
that are fluid
situational ethical
thought up in the moment
bars on the windows

who can I kiss
who can I hug
who do a bow to
when do I shrug

is there space
for breath to pass
is there place
where I can rest

where am I safe
where I am I free
where does worry
hover or flee

How is it Such Beauty Brings So Much Pain?

mowing around wild flowers

I have lyre-leaf sage pushing up
blue purple blooms
and lots of fleabane
little daisies with delicate white petals
and yellow centers to attract all the bees
and butterflies

the grass had grown deep
and I was reluctant to cut it
with all the dandelions and violets
a million little lavender blooms
but it was on the verge . . .

I pushed my electric mower
out of the garage
fiddled with it until it started
and ran it until the battery died
tomorrow I will finish

cut the back yard paths
and patches
and leave prairies
for the wild things
that come and go

the pollen I stirred up
was more than my body could handle
I ache, that is what my body does
with pollen
I ache

and when I do lament
is just around the corner
I know it is just physical
but I cannot draw the boundary
I lament that I ache and I ache
my lamentation

were it a song to heaven
I would sing to the gods
in a raspy voice
how is it such beauty
brings so much pain

how is it such beauty
brings so much pain

how it is such beauty
brings so much pain

HYMN FOR A FULL DAY

I am often asked
are you retired
and it is like the question
are you in a relationship
and my answer
it is complicated
is the best
I can do

today I had seven appointments
each of them challenging
in myriad ways
some in person
some online
and some by phone
I had half an hour break
in the morning
and an hour in the afternoon
to eat and stretch
to pet the cats

yesterday it was five
but none the day before
and only one tomorrow
am I retired?

I am on Saturday and Sunday
mostly on Monday
and on the days when work is light
I visit my therapists
who keep the coffee
percolating

who knit the tears
in the seams

and I see friends
for dinner, lunch
and breakfast
not so much for walks
it is humid Summer
in Atlanta
80 degrees
at 8 AM

tonight
the frog orchestra
is writing a new symphony
in my back garden
my cats are lolling
and I have turned off the news
not out of indifference
so much trauma
so much sadness
but hasn't music
always gotten us through?
I have hundreds of albums
cassette tapes and CD's
I love music
but it is the frogs
singing in my forest
that bring me peace
through quiet
and crescendo
rising and falling
rising and falling
the arc and ebb
of being

everlasting
exquisitely fragile
and I yield to wonder
and muster
gratitude
oh beautiful evening
oh life everflowing
oh wonder unfolding
oh glory divine

I Am A Lucky Guy

another reprieve

my first client emailed yesterday
his young children had been sick . . .
I replied I hope they are better soon
and my gardener, postponer supreme
postponed
so the cats and I slept in
Zephyr in the crook of my knees
and Ferdinand on the blanket
at the foot of the bed
and I had time to make a run
for kitty litter
and milk
and frozen waffles

everyone came in person today
a new client
an ongoing client
and an old client
from a dozen years ago
and I was reminded
about the power of narrative
how we weave in and out
of each others stories
I am their Yoda
with smaller cars
and human skin
and much less cosmic wisdom
but with hard won human
common sense

I got to change the cat litter
and brush the cats
(their new addiction)
cut some flowers
put magic potions
on my right knee
and take a thirty minute nap

I met one of my dearest, oldest friends
Ilene at Wahoo! a nearby restaurant
and we sat outside
and she had a fancy Manhattan
and I had a vodka martini straight up
with a twist
we shared pimento cheese fritters
and I had fried chicken, mashed potatoes
and collard greens, comfort food
and she had a steak medium rare
with risotto and asparagus
we wisely declined dessert

she talked about her trip with her sister Judi
to Montreal
and I talked about my week in Nashville
caring for my father
and the rest of what we talked about
is classified
not for legal or moral reasons
we are both psychotherapists
with a hundred years of experience between us
one of life's great lessons
is discernment

there are two bodhisattvas
that flank the Buddha

My Ordinary Life

the most popular one is Kuan Yin
Avalokiteshvara
the Bodhisattva of Compassion
but on the other side
is Mansushri
"Gentle Wisdom"
the Bodhisattva of Discernment
who wields a very sharp saber

so what I can't say is as important
as what I can say
what I don't do
is as important
as what I do do

it began raining as we were finishing
and we were sitting in the garden
and felt the sprinkle
Ilene treated me
she's a doll
and we both walked out
to find our valet
under an umbrella
our cars were right there
Ilene paid him
and took her keys
no need for him to get wetter
and I did too
and told him I did not recognize
his accent
Togo he said
and I said I had been to Ghana
but not to Togo
next door he said
we both smiled

I tipped him more
and told him stay dry
as I took my keys
and walked through the rain
to my nearby car
and drove home
stomach full
heart happy

I am a lucky guy

I Am Here

some days I almost disappear
I don't go out
I don't leave the small perimeter of my
home and garden
I see no one but the cats
who if they could would
disappear with me

I may see clients virtually
speak to friends by phone
answer emails or messages
but I dine alone

I go as far as my mailbox
but the mail is of no concern
no packages are delivered
no branches have fallen
in my smaller world

the moss is one more shade of green
the birds have eaten half the seed
I have left them

I picked another lavender camellia
for the vase beside the portal
that is my laptop computer

and here I write about cats
and my simple lunch
and here I wait
for a signal
that it is safe
all clear

but until
I hear
I am here

I Cooked Breakfast With My Friend Paul This Morning

he said what can I do
and I told him to crack and scramble the eggs
I told him to stir slow like the French
who like soft eggs
and he did

the eggs, the grits and the Italian sausage
lined up and fed us
gave us energy to talk

he said he had to meet his sister for biscuits
and we had an exquisite hug
I hope those were some good biscuits
I needed an early nap

Paul is 27 and I am 71
he is finishing medical school
and waiting to be selected for a residency
in anesthesia

he is growing naturally
and naturally I am diminishing
I tell him I have hope in the future
and he whispers don't die
don't die for decades

neither of us are sure
that the magic of his medicine
will be the magic
we both pray for

in nineteen years I will be ninety
should I be so lucky
and I will sit in one of the posh chairs
in my parlor
and Paul will take my picture

and if this is so
I promise a wink
tilting my head
and maybe I'll blow a kiss

It Should Have Been A Good Day

"follow your own weird"
     – James Broughton

the autumn leaves were falling
the sky was blue and a breeze was blowing
I had lunch with a dear friend
at a favorite restaurant
and went to a cherished museum
to visit 'old friends' in the collection
and see an amazing new exhibit

my feline companions have been
especially sweet
and there has been plenty of good food
to eat
and I took a long nap
with a heating pad on warm
to ease my back

and yes the darkness came sooner
it is that time in the calendar
and yes I had invitations
to share warmth
that were clear and very dear

there was something I couldn't shake
was it a shudder or a fear
or the darkening time of year
or something dreadful coming near

my cats reassured me
with lots of snuggles
and purrs
that maybe I am just weird

it is okay
it is normally abnormal
it is occasionally expected
to be weird

it was a good day
it was a good day
to be weird
to be weird

It Wasn't An Easy Morning

and I didn't want to get up early
but I needed to coordinate with an editor
and a doctor
so I pushed myself to arise
and make coffee
and rewarded myself
with whipped cream
for my dark roasted
Ethiopian brew

as the coffee was brewing
I was opening blinds
and opening the front door
when I spied something
awry
the trash can I set out
last night for today's pick up
was on its side
and its contents
well I couldn't see exactly
so I put on my street shoes
and went out
and it was a mess
I got my garden gloves
and a bigger trash bag
and cleaned it up
so the truck that forgot to come by
would not have to mess
with a mess

I came back inside
washed my gloves

and got my first sip
bitter and creamy
and that distracted me
I could read the news
and catch up on social media
and not think about
the next thing I didn't want to do

it wasn't an easy decision
and I did not want to be first in line
but I wanted protection
and I know it comes too rarely
to too few

I am not a front line health care worker
or a sex worker or a young person
in a never-ending struggle with my hormones
but I am not ready for the cloister
and I cannot not remember
the disease that scared me
the plague that scarred me
and for more than a decade
would have killed me
and there is still no vaccine
still no vaccine

it was easier and quicker than
I imagined
I signed up online
and four days later
I arrived on time
at the DeKalb County Health Department
housed in a pretty brick building
just this side of the Charlie Brown Airport
easy parking

easy entry
I signed in and was asked to sanitize
my hands
I was directed down a long hallway
asked to sign in again
given a form to fill out and sign
it had the number 17 on it
so I knew my place in line
I sat in a waiting area
with 20 others assigned this time
I may have been the oldest
but there were other silver hairs
about half Black and half white and Asian
only one female
only one fellow not wearing a mask
I waited

when my name was called
I followed a nurse down another corridor
into an exam room
and she asked a couple of questions
to make sure I was not in danger
and then I put my left arm
on the table beside her
and she injected my lower inner arm
between the layers of skin
it didn't hurt but wasn't pleasant
she said, there
that's your mosquito bite
and that's what it resembled
I waited fifteen minutes more
just like after Covid vaccines
to make sure I didn't react
and then was given an appointment

for my second shot
exactly a month from today

I felt a little stoned
but not out of it
more like I was walking out of a Dali
painting and back to my car in the parking lot
I turned right, the wrong way, on purpose
and drove past the airport entrance
and a little further down
turned into a side street
and reversed my direction
I stopped for gas
and then at a jewelry store
to ask about repairs
and met a friend for lunch
in a pleasant little restaurant
he said how are you
and I said half drunk
and told him about my morning

after lunch and another errand
I am on Skype with a client
listening to myself as I give him a pep talk
speaking to him in his native tongue
and translating back
into my own voice
saying let fear (the devil) go
and let love and light
(your higher power)
hold you

after we said goodbye
I learned another friend has died
I spoke to her yesterday by phone

another friend at her bedside
told me she can hear you
and I spoke to her in her language
wishing her comfort
and comfort came early this afternoon

I sat on my neighbors' porch visiting
with, I won't call her a cat sitter,
perhaps a cat whisperer
about her project to re-create
an erased community
and felt myself tearful
if you have read this far
you need not imagine why

I told my client in his language
to recite the 23rd Psalm
when he needed reassurance
and to take a deep breath
and count to 4

one
two
three

four

I Was Still Sleeping

when I heard a tentative knock on my door
I looked at my phone
and my gardener had texted
I will be there at 8
it was 8:30
so I got up and put on my shorts
and t-shirt and answered the door
and invited him in
I had replaced the old weed whacker
with a new one
and asked him
to assemble it
while I got dressed
in clothes
that discourage mosquitoes

my gardener
Robin is his name
works at triple speed
I am amazed
at how much he does
in a small frame
of time

he had already weeded
the beds in my front garden
and within an hour he cut
the grass in my gardens
front and back
sparing
(I am an eccentric)
my favorite weeds

his endeavor inspires mine
and I am out
enduring heat
and bug bites
getting little things done
touching up my car
watering and trimming
and guiding him
to trim branches
overhanging my house

he mulches
I cut zinnias
and when he leaves
I finish
put seed in the birdfeeder
replenish the water
in the birdbath
bring in the tools
lock the garden gate
and spray Bad Bone Water
on my insect bits
just like I did for him

I have biting flies
and he had a bad bite on his back
and the Bad Bone Water
made it so much better
so I knew to use it
on my back too
I had more stings
more venom

I allowed myself
time to cool

before I showered
and took a nap

some naps are easier
to arise from
this was a long nap
much needed

when I arose
it was time to cook dinner
and I did
it is routine
make the salad
cook the grain
prepare the protein

my friend Kilian was coming for dinner
I had not seen him in a month
so there was lots to catch up on
we wandered, as we always do
over hill and vale
covering the stuff of life
and we parted on my steps
hours later
talking about sex

he is young
and eros is insistent
I am no longer young
and eros is an afterthought
I told him
I had mourned the loss
and he said you are the lucky one
and we both agreed
the equation changes

I don't want not to be kissed
I don't want not to be held
I don't want to lose bliss
or anything profound

but tonight
alone
I don't miss
the compromise
of company

I had a lovely dinner
with a lovely friend
where love is never a question
but a certainty
and I have the company of cats
where love is never a question
always on their terms and sublime
and my fingers type
in the rhythm of life
and love is never a question

I Want To Be Better Than I Pretend To Be

I want to be more loving, more patient
more compassionate, more understanding
and certainly more forgiving

it is like being honest in physical therapy
my sweet PT
understands
I was a little grandiose
in how many repetitions
of how many exercises
I could do

I have discovered
that there is enough time
for me to stop
at a really good donut shop between
physical therapy
and chiropractic
I order two glazed donuts
after trying all the fancy ones
I am reduced to the simplicity
of my first Krispy Kremes
fried dough
glazed in sugar
melts in my mouth
I get two donuts
and two donut holes
I eat the holes and save the donuts
one for reward
for taxing my body

and one as a promise
to wake up with a smile tomorrow

on my way home
I get a deli sandwich
I just want someone else
to make my lunch
and I buy white cherries
expensive
but another reward

I eat half the sandwich
do couples therapy on Skype
eat the other half
and have a donut
and dispatch myself
to the farmer's market

the DeKalb Farmers Market
ten minutes from my house
is one of the Seven Wonders of Atlanta
sprawling, full of every vegetable, fruit and herb
always fresh
but not a farmer's market
no farmers selling their harvest
but an employer of hundreds
of recent immigrants and refugees
and shopped in by every kind of person
who lives in our metropolitan region
I buy coffee from India
house-baked bran muffins
lemons from Mexico
domestic cow feta cheese
and wheat grass for the cats
and radish sprouts for my salad

I was dog tired when I got home
and as always a part of my mind
turns to infection
I am using hand sanitizer again
after a physician told me
you can get monkeypox from touching things
thirty minutes on my futon bed
with the ceiling fan
whirling overhead
and I am ready to call a friend
and we commiserate
he about an awful tooth extraction
me about my knee
which did not miraculously
stop complaining after a cortisol shot
and I admit defeat
there is no medical miracle
no doctor who can make me young again

my healing is up to me
and yes, I can find wonderful help
my kind and competent chiropractor
my kind and competent acupuncturist
my kind and competent physical therapist
my kind and competent and long-time physician
and I am better for all their kindness
and their expertise
but I am still a person getting older in a body
dodging a pandemic or maybe two
wary of the world and all its consequences
and wanting and wanting ease

in the end it is I who must find comfort
and some of that comfort
comes in rest and rest alone

My Ordinary Life

the energy consumed by worry
has not made me better
it is a leak that's hard to plug
I was schooled in Boy Scout philosophy
"Be Prepared"

I believe in seat belts
condoms
brushing my teeth
and having insurance

I lock my doors
and check my blood pressure
brush my cats
and have my car's oil changed

if I were religious
I would say prayers
ring bells
and light incense

I don't have those consolations
but I do know nature looks back at me
that I have so many trees
(and friends) I can lean on
I know my cats have wisdom
and check on me
sit beside my knee
or want rest upon my chest
above my heart

I know I need to try
but I also need to let things pass by
I have been sitting on the river bank
long enough
to trust the flow
what goes, what comes around

I SAY YES

I have always been
ambivalent
I will fight death
like I fought birth
I will fight love
like I fought loss
if I were the waters
of the sea
I would be churning
if I were a forest
I would be burning
if I were a cloud
I would be turning
into a storm

I have studied
the path of contemplation
sat myself down
on the cushion of meditation
whirled and howled
kept my head up
and drowned
in emotion

I have been the last leaf
to fall
and the first daffodil
I am short
and I am tall
young as tomorrow
and old as yesterday

I still want a kiss
to lay my head upon

your shoulder
and I shudder
when I touch
mortal flesh

this is not a cry for pity
for I have had my part
more than plenty
and I will wake again
take the first breath
of morning
and dance another day

I hear the mermaids singing
I feel the angels winging
and the fairies tickle
my fingers and my toes

the next eruption
may entomb me in lava
the next great wave
may sweep me away
the next tornado
may lift me up
to heaven
but it is more likely
to be my fate
that one morning
I awake
and the light
overtakes me
and opens up
above me
and I am given
one more choice
and I say yes

I Put Myself
On A Point System

I put myself on a point system
like Weight Watchers only these points
are similar to being in a war zone
and going out for food or medicine

I can go for groceries once a week
if I go at the right time
I check the parking lot of the grocery store
and if it is full I go home

today I mailed packages
and tried to fax some documents
the packages went out
the fax failed. not happy about that.

Zero points for Zoom
like vegetables
I can have all the Zoom
I want
like celery
and though I like celery
and purchase it when I spend points for groceries
the peanut M and M's I purchased at Fed Ex
where I shipped my packages
and was confounded in my faxing
were only slightly consoling

I spent 3 hours on a Zoom conference this evening
and although it is better than nothing
I could not smell or taste anyone

I could feel no compression of arms around my body
I could speak and listen and wish everyone well
and I did

it was celery
and I wanted sweet potatoes
with lots of butter
sweet potatoes
that smelled like cinnamon
sweet potatoes
that peeled away from their skin
and were roasted to caramel
and sat warm in my belly

tomorrow I will bake
sweet potatoes
sprinkled with cinnamon
and dressed with butter
I will peel the flesh from the skin
and dive in

no points to count
no love to doubt

ICARUS

hope is a thing with feathers*
so when I see a bird fly high
like Emily, I have hope
hope is a falling leaf
that doesn't just drop
but floats on the wind
like the leaves of the trees
I let go of fear
and hope
I will float

every night
I prepare for sleep
make sure the doors are locked
and my cats and I are safe
in our castle keep
every morning
I open my eyes
put one foot on the floor
and then the other
and I rise

I hope today will be
the day
I realize

I can fly

* Emily Dickenson

IMMUNITY

two weeks ago
I had my second shot
the vaccine hurt my arm
and made me a little sick
and a little tired
on the third day
I was okay

yesterday I had my hair cut
for the first time in a year
today I shopped in two places
almost without fear

what will I do tomorrow
will I sit in the sunshine
walk in the park
hold my breath
and wait until dark

a year alone and apart
has had its lessons
more about what I don't
than what I do

I don't take for
granted simple services
I don't wait for dreams
to come true

and yet I do
I know push increases push
and patience
increases patience

I feel the pull
and know the push
I wait for the echo
that bounces off a star

I get a gold medal
for a year of being careful
and a haircut
nothing special

special

INTUITION

when I was younger
I spent a lot of time
with psychics
I learned to read the Tarot
and later mastered the Runes
I would carry my Rune bag
 whenever I traveled
I would read for myself
should I go East or West
prowl or rest

reading for others
was my litmus test
I would have them pull runes
from the bag
until we had a happy ending
one fellow pulled fourteen
he was up to no good and may still be
digging himself out
thirty years later

I could pull a rune right now
and it would give me an answer
I have learned as I've grown older
an answer is only the prelude
to the next question

and if life is forever enfolding
answers in questions
and questions in answers
maybe it is best not to know
because knowledge

is always the prelude
to confusion

"it is the law of heaven
to lessen the redundant
and fill up the insufficient"
the only lines I know by heart
from the I-Ching
the only lines I know by heart
from the Bible
"Jesus wept"

what I don't know
about the tears of the Messiah
are they of sorrow
or joy
are they of sorrow
or joy

Jesus wept

INSOMNIA

not sure why I am awake at 2:30
sometimes I stir briefly at 4
not sure why I found sleep elusive
or who put on the soundtrack
of catastrophe
which lasted as long as an opera

I rarely get up
much less turn a light on
much less the laptop
I tried to dope myself
with a sweet drink
ibuprofen and an antihistamine

back in the dark of my bed
strange images swirled in my head
everything from romantic disappointment
to international intrigue
I told myself to breathe
and I would take one breath
and one breath more
before the maelstrom
pulled me under

my cats tag teamed me
one would curl beside me
and the other in turn
would rest on my thigh
I was purred over
the way cats pray

finally the chord of discord
was severed

and I like a little boat
drifted down the river

the alarm, a rarely-used device
woke me up
I had appointments
and I roused my somnolent self
made coffee
and set sail for a new day
floating past the mists
of despair
to where my destiny
was waiting

KNEE

to take a knee
is radical
necessary
unifying
sacrificing
and everyday
a plumber takes a knee
a carpenter
a polisher of marble
an emergency medical technician
a soldier
takes a knee

my knee in trouble
is my right knee
my driving knee
my physical therapist
tells me don't drive
with an aching knee
don't drive for hours
with an aching knee

my acupuncturist
surrounds the ache in my knee
with her tiny needles
it doesn't ache
I drive home
and the ache slowly returns
four ibuprofen later
I stop feeling it
for four hours
and now it aches again

and more ibuprofen later
my knee will relax with me
into the vale of sleep

peace will be my pillow
until inflammation moves me
to move
and reminds me that in the love of life
is its ache

my knee teaches me
with its throb
I am still full of life
my heart fuels the beat
my pain is just the reverb
that makes movement
meaningful
so here's to life
and all its aches
and joys
here's to life

Keats at 200

Adieu! the fancy cannot cheat so well
As she is fam'd to do, deceiving elf.

everyone in England was sick
and everyone in Ireland was dying

after a bitter separation I fled for the holidays
Christmas in Ireland and New Year's in London
seemed like a good way to balm my heart

my friends in Dublin and London were welcoming
and I felt balmed indeed by their hospitality
the weather was much less hospitable
the wind blew sideways
a constant drizzle or rain
the sun never shone

it is true that the temperature there
was similar to my home in Atlanta
but wind and rain and darkness
from four in the afternoon until ten in the morning
were not what my aching heart needed
oh no

my first outing in Dublin was to an odd
 funeral of a woman friend of the couple
I stayed with
she was an unhappy alcoholic
who drank herself into an early grave
she had decided against her Catholic faith
not to be buried
but cremated

at the time cremation was unusual in Ireland
and the chapel for the service was cold as ice
rented out in quarter-hour intervals
one group was herded in
as the last was herded out

there was a eulogy not by a priest
that I can't remember
but what stands out twenty-five years later
was the conveyor belt that carried her casket
through a velvet curtain
into the flames

I had not visited London before
my trip to celebrate the New Year
I stayed with a brilliant mathematician
who lived in a flat off Hampstead Heath
where George Orwell, according to a plaque
had written 1984

my friend Daniel had a penchant for damsels in distress
so when his friend Lady Deborah cried out for help
after breaking her leg in a skiing accident in Switzerland
I had to give up my cozy bed
for a tiny bedroom on the porch
where servants had slept
without the comfort of heat

we did celebrate the new year
at a fancy Chinese restaurant
that served Peking duck
and I did go to the British Museum
and marvel at the stolen Elgin Marbles
I saw the genius of Blake at the Tate

and the bric-a-brac of the Empire
at the Victoria and Albert

because of proximity I visited the Freud Museum
and saw the mother couch and all of Sigmund's
ancient Greek, Roman and Egyptian statuettes
and I visited the Keats House
where the divine poet had been a lodger
before he went to Rome and died
he wrote Ode to a Nightingale there

I saw his death mask
and the ring he offered to his beloved Fanny Brawn
he wrote the ode in the garden
while his cheeks still glowed
before tuberculosis sent him south to Rome
to die young and beautiful
Keats was the prototype
for James Dean and Jean-Michel Basquiat
Jim Morrison and Jimmy Hendricks
had they lived would their magic have waned
Keats was only twenty-five
born two hundred years ago
and still alive

JAWS

I am mostly unaware of my jaws
they do their work with precision
they push my upper teeth
into my lower teeth
and grind my food
so I can swallow

when they lock and strain
I become the Tin Man
in search of an oil can
I wince at the clinch
I cannot but notice
when they pop
like rubber bands

when I fill out the form
for my next acupuncture treatment
I note that I have tension
just that

my acupuncturist
tells me that the stomach
metaphorically digests everything
all the food and all the mood
and all the information
and the jaw
chews and chews
and chews

I never know where she will insert
the tiny needles or if I will feel a thing
9 times out of 10 I don't

and the 10th time
I might say she hits a nerve
I feel a jolt
just for a second
but that second tells me
a key is being inserted into a lock
and a lock is turning slowly
and a channel is opening

I count the needles
left and right jaw
left and right wrist
left and right knee
third eye
and I hear her talking
about taking just one breath
and releasing
and it is as if
I am underwater
except for my taking
one breath
releasing
and slowly rising
to the surface
of my being

she takes my pulses
and tells me my body
has released
and gently tells me
in words I can hardly hear
not to hold on
not to tighten
not to take on
not to frighten myself

how do I float
in the womb of the cosmos
how to let go of how
and float in the womb of the cosmos
letting go of another breath
letting go of life and death

LET THE FOREST HEAL ME

a back porch visit
good coffee
goldfinches feeding off dried
echinacea seeds
conversing about what was
imagining vacations
not talking about the news

shopping
I love to shop for food
I love to cook
this afternoon
I made cold cucumber soup
I will serve for dinner tomorrow
and a sautee of scallops
and onions and dill
I ate for my supper

I spoke on the phone with an old friend
and would have dialed more numbers
but mostly I wanted to rest
put aside ambition
let my spirit ramble
oh how I love to ramble

the dishes are clean
and back in their places
a stick of incense
sacred to Saraswati
has replaced
the smell of supper
and I am in my quiet home

with my treefrog and cicada orchestra
warming up
and my cats having had their dinner
in deep contentment
I had planned this night
to be one of solitude
the only book to read
is my own thoughts
and as I listen to the orchestra
in my trees
I might just find me
an aria to sing
or I might
just swaddle myself
and let the forest
heal me

LUMINOUS

my friend Noël
came for dinner
and I admit
I invite him
because
he is luminous

two years ago
Noël fell from the roof
of his house
and was told by doctors
he would not walk again

he drove to my house
walked to my door
and climbed my steps
we sat in my parlor
and had a drink
told stories
and ate dinner together

we see each other's luminosity
in heightened states
extreme emergency
extreme ecstasy

Noël has been putting his broken body
back together
bone by bone
tendon by tendon

what does my body do
across the table from his body
across narratives
and under sinew

how do my neurons
rearrange themselves
to accept his transmissions
and send clear signals

I suppose since we are broken
in different ways my brokenness
speaks to him and his to me
it is only through the cracks in the egg
we see

MAKE ART

we are all in grief

cross your heart if you have suffered from Covid or had a
loved one who suffered and died and do this invisibly if you
have a need to be private
cross your heart
in solidarity with everyone who has suffered a loss of liberty
or life
did not attend a prom or go on a senior trip
or who missed a holiday or was denied a memorial for a
loved one
cross your heart
if you are weary and frightened
and are Zoomed and Skyped out of your mind
if you are scared to re-enter the world
if you are immunocompromised
or living with someone
with comorbidities like organ transplant
diabetes, HIV or just plain old age

if we were paying attention
we have been scared to death
and scarred by fear
and it isn't over yet
each of us calculates again and again
whether it is Covid or skin
where do we walk
how do we move
as if the needle on the groove
of our existence
might hop and skip

this is not just about a wanton virus
this is about Breonna, Treyvon, Antoine, George Floyd
it is about trans and Asian victims of hate crimes
it is about the energy it takes
to walk through the minefields
of virus, racism, sexism, homophobia
it is how we cope with fear
how we keep ourselves safe
and how we write a letter or a song
or make a film or paint a painting
that will save our spirits
and flash a warning of encouragement
to future generations
be strong be smart
make art
be strong be smart
make art
set the record
testify
we are here
life is dear
and we are more together
than we are apart

Making Cornbread For Friends

when I make it for myself
I go the simple route
just self-rising cornmeal
buttermilk and oil in the pan

when I am making it for friends
I add cut corn, add an egg
and decorate with sage leaves
from my garden

what I like is the crunch
I can never get right on purpose
my mother could
in the footsteps of my grandmothers

my Nana cooked it for every lunch and dinner
the aroma from the stove was the signal
we would eat in twenty minutes
she cooked it in a cast iron skillet
and flipped it
with her ninety-eight year old hand
and it was perfect and crunchy
and moist on the inside
waiting for the butter

aren't we all waiting for the butter
aren't we all waiting to melt
and sit beside the turnip greens
and field peas

My Ordinary Life

a little bite of this
a little bite of that
and cornbread
cornbread

Missing Martha

heavy hearts

call it a celebration of life
or a memorial service
or a last rite
say she lived a long full life
that in the end her body was her burden
and death a mercy
share stories poignant and funny
sing meaningful songs
read her dead wife's poetry
about the mystery, the mystery
hear a nephew review
their history of shared culinary delights
recognize her caregivers as angels
listen to her neighbors who loved her
look upon the gorgeous floral arrangement
in white and purple
share hello hugs
in masks, faces turned aside
walk down the steep stairs to the sidewalk
slowly holding on to the rail
drive home a different way
arrive hungry
warm leftovers
make a salad
try to eat, hungry but half an appetite
what is missing

Martha

and our hearts are heavy
such is grief
no matter the how and when
who was there and who was not
how lovely it all was
how loving we all were with each other
our hearts are heavy

missing Martha

in memory of Martha Renfroe Garner

My Shining Ride

Abrihaman picked me up a little after 4
this afternoon
and took me to Decatur Collision
where Lazar B showed me
my new bumper
and took my debit card

my twenty-year-old car
a gift, a silver Lexus SC 430
had been reborn
like a painting restored

I keep the car
because it is a work of art
reliable transportation
and a meditation
on speed in motion

the bumper
contained the evidence
or all my mistakes
pulling up too far
too wide
bump, bump, bump

I feel like I have
gone to Confession
and for a tidy sum
been absolved of my sins

Abrihaman who came from Somalia
when he was twelve

has just graduated from Georgia State
with a business degree
was in Somali attire
a long shiny salmon colored shirt
over white trousers
a sculpted beard
we talked about Stone Mountain
where I used to live
and he lives now
and the Somali mosque
nearby

Lazer did not share much story
but moved a black SUV
so I could gracefully back
my polished beauty out
of his parking lot
and enjoy the air conditioning
at full blast
until my moment of truth
when I pushed the button
and my garage door opened
and I skillfully parked
my shining ride
in the dark of my garage

My Oh My

so old friends gather
for a celebration of life
a Sunday service
and my friend Don
gives the talk
about "the bucket list"

it is senior shorthand
for what you want to do
before it's too late
and at the end of his talk
he asked the gathered friends
what is important

now most of us are 70+
and friend Linda said
she had heard from the NY Times
they accepted her letter to the editor
one friend said she wanted grandchildren
another said he had been learning Spanish
and could speak it with increasing proficiency
and another spoke poingantly about bearing witness
to the Holocaust at Auschwitz
no one said they wanted to see the Pyramids
(Don is headed to the Parthenon)
or climb a tall mountain
or swim a wide river

septuagenarians have a different wish list
that grows more specific
as we enter our '80's and '90's
I want to see my old friend Martha Lou
I want to visit my old friend the Maharaja

and my second family in Africa
I'd like to go back to Chicago's Art Institute
and Niagara Falls and ride on the Maid of the Mist
maybe I can record more music
write more poems
witness more sunrise/sunset
listen as I did this afternoon
to a rainstorm watering my garden
go to another movie, see another play
attend another concert
eat more farm-to-table gourmet
and learn more history

I am becoming history
I am the one who
once upon a time
saw my first butterfly
flutter by
heard my first ocean wave
and saw my first condor
soaring over
grandeur
watched the sun set
on the Taj Mahal

I know there will be more marvels
but I know as well
that each dinner with a friend
is a gift
each laugh
each lament
each sigh
is a treasure
I won't remember
when it is my turn

to fly away
and say goodbye
another day
a final sigh
but what a life
my oh my

My Father, 93, Rearranges The Universe

something always needs moving
to make more space
to be convenient
to keep from falling
my father studies his world
with his engineer's eyes
and his sense of place
where do you place
a wrench, a screwdriver
an awl, your wallet
your keys

and then there is the dilemma of time
you know when the sky fills up with light
to rise
and after darkness falls
and you wait in the quiet night
to find the path to bed

when light begins again
you rise
and walk to the front door
open it
and find the newspaper
in its thin plastic wrapper
you make coffee
and oatmeal in the microwave
and read the paper slowly
work the sudoku as best as you can
contemplate the advice of Ann Landers

and shake your head about the sorry state
of affairs that the world has come to
you feed the cat and open the blinds
so the cat can see the birds
that come to the feeders
and they do

and then it is time to rearrange the world again
maybe this should be there instead of here
and where is that that should be there
and time disappears until the telephone rings
and where is the telephone
and who is that voice
that says hello, hello

hello and there you go
if it is a friend you are friendly
if it is a request for donation
you are friendly but provide no information
every time you have it caused consternation
and a flurry of activity by your children
who say oh no

and then you go
to look for something lost
that can't be found
your wife finally left you
for god
your memory betrays you
and isn't around
your bladder won't be subdued
you pee and pee
your balance is now in full falter
and what is there to do

but rearrange what you have rearranged
again, to stop where you begin
and begin and begin and begin
and like a wheel
you make the universe spin

MOTHER

mother
is there a bigger word?
not even god
is as big as mother

we have many gods
and one mother

she was our harbor
our safe beginning
no matter the rest of the story
her womb is prologue

did she love us or rue us
was she sacred or profane
did she die early or rule us
regardless we're not the same

if she loved us was it too much
or too little, too long or too short
if she didn't how did it wound us
how did we survive for breath to report

and what can we say by way of thanks
for a blood sacrifice, her risking her life
how many roses comfort a grave
how many candles are ever enough

is her absence a cave
we can curl into
and wait out the seasons
until our absence

folds into hers

mother

MILAGRO

my father repeats his intention
to follow my mother into death
this of course provided
he cannot find remediation
for his curse

I say I understand
I offer to find a shrine
or a holy well
where he can leave
an image of his problem
milagro
in care of a saint

I do not think a doctor can help him
I do not think he can help himself
I will not force nutrition
if he like she
decides no more

and what heaven will do with him
or me or anybody
is a mystery

tonight my prayer
is a little prayer
may he be free
of suffering
that I may pray
this prayer
no more

milagro

MIKE THE BUG MAN

is six feet tall and always in a light blue cap
he is an independent exterminator
a Viet Nam vet and 79 on his last birthday

Mike is one of my favorite people
not only because he sets traps for rats
with peanut butter in my attic and garage
and dusts for roaches and sprays around my house
sending a signal to spiders

Mike has a story and he is telling me
about his life, one of thirteen children
he consoles me on the death of my mother
and we do the math, his mother died at 63
he says he hated his father
his father beat his mother
impregnated her and beat her
and Mike says when he became a Christian
he had to repent
he had to let go of his hatred

he said it was time to bring our troops
home from Afghanistan
he said it is so awful here
how could we be elsewhere
he said we have to take care of our own

and I with my soft hands
and remote compassion
think of the fall of Saigon
and wonder who will protect the women
and children and the queerfolk

when the hateful Taliban overrun
Kabul and Kandahar
will there be tent cities
in the backyards of Bush, Cheney and the Clintons
will Barack and Michelle
be serving soup in my garden
will those who flee medieval morality
be given a space
to raise bees and corn and tomatoes
and sleep at night

and sleep at night
and sleep at night
free of fear
free of fear

free

homage to Michael Hamilton

MAYBE

I watched the inauguration
with tears streaming down my cheeks
not for what President Biden said
or his beautiful young poet
or Lady Gaga in her frills
with her perfect pitch
I was not crying for Kamala Harris
our most-beautiful-ever vice-president
or the hero who escorted her
or all the former presidents and first ladies
or the second gentleman
or the flags on the mall
or the Marine band in full flare
or Garth Brooks' Amazing Grace
nor the priest or the preacher
I was not moved by a single word
or note
I was in tears because my ears
were hearing words in earnest
and I have survived the mistakes
and unrest and willful evil
that has bedeviled my dreams
and killed hundreds of thousands

it was as if the radio signal
that had blasted hate and chaos
had gone silent
and a radio signal that broadcast
decency, hope and a little bit of grace
was breaking through

maybe I can come out of the shelter
maybe the bombs have stopped dropping
maybe it is okay
to say I love you
again

maybe I can breathe
full and free

maybe there is a future
for you and me

On Point

the battery in my alarm clock
must be weak
it did not tweak
much less alarm

I was hosting two fellow poets
and preparing for two renovators
and I decided
to make the coffee
and take the shower
and sure enough
after I backed my car onto the street
and opened the garden gate
I heard commotion
and my fix-it friends were on site
and my poet friends would have appetite
and so I drove to the Indian village
a couple of miles from my house
and bought samosas and friend peppers
for all of us

my friend Rupert
shared a poem about
watching a bi-plane
fly around Stone Mountain
and my friend Dan
shared a poem
about an encounter
with a barracuda

we ate samosas
and fried peppers

while Mario and Mario
were fixing my gutters
and the bricks in my
driveway
and eating samosas
and fried peppers

Rupert indulged
in a flight of fantasy
imagining lovers
in long scarves
in an ancient plane
that helped them
come closer
to the illusion
of a bigger moon

Dan had floated
beyond the lagoon
with the tiny silver fish
and unwittingly
encountered
a razor toothed demon
of the deeper seas

and I was lamenting
honestly
I was lamenting
my grief
not my loss
a motherless child

and Mario and Mario
were cementing
old bricks and securing
new gutters
and we were all united
by geography
and samosas
and the time
between one and three
when the five of us
were hammering away
at reality

OUR VERY DIFFERENT HEARTS

if we could just slow down
I think of that when a car
is passing me in traffic on the right
and weaving in and out
and we arrive at the same time
at the same stop light
if we could just slow down

we are all going to the same
resting place
why be in a hurry?
only fate knows our arrival time
and *tempus fugit*
fate
holds the stopwatch

I think of the environment
and how it is getting hotter
and dryer
but tonight in my garden
it is moist and cool
and the frog orchestra
is sweet as Chopin
and bright as Bach
and there is thunder

if we could turn politics
into poetry
what would we sustain
and what would be refrain
and what would echo
would there be moments

of blunder
of communion?

I am making chili
and cooking it slow
I can smell the cumin
and the onions
and understand
they are meeting the beans
and speaking in rosemary
and waiting for the cheese
and sour cream

my Thai Buddhist monk friend
Ruangvit
asked me if I was in
a "hurry up"
and invited me to sit with him
under the shade of a tree
and share a cigarette

he told me he was called
"The Iron Monk"
because he walked
all the way across Thailand
he was handsome
and only twenty-five
he showed me
the city temples
and the forest temple
in Chiang Mai
and respecting his custom
I did not eat during the day
only breakfast and after dusk
dinner

we wrote to each other
for several years
and then
living on a spinning planet
we spun away
the man in the photograph
I took of my friend
may be a spirit
or an elder monk
or perhaps he followed
a different play

had I been
in a "hurry up"
we would never have
shared a cigarette
or midday hunger
or the wonder
as we were taking
each other
into our very different
hearts

OWLS AND ELEPHANTS

these were Naunie's totem
animals
along with small dogs
Paco and Elsie

Naunie had a garden
on the side of her house
and in good years
got tomatoes
and peppers
and beans

she had a grandson
she referred to
as Butterbean
a term of endearment
and she always
doted
over what he said
and did

after Butterbean
came the twin ballerinas
Naunie had been a dancer
and a majorette in her youth
only an accident had slowed her down

like a butterfly with a broken wing
she was captured by a handsome
bird of prey
she became an Air Force wife
who lived half her married life
above the Arctic Circle

how she became Atlanta's premier psychic
is foggy to me
I think it was foggy to her
how does a caterpillar
become a butterfly
Naunie drew on past
experience

she was bold and beautiful
and envied and feared
legend has it
when she was tried for heresy
by the Foundation of Truth
she became so angry
that a chair was flung across the room
by unseen hands

like for everyone else
there was a banana peel
in Naunie's destiny
as there is in yours
and mine
if you've seen your last
banana peel
write your will

and she slipped
and it hurt
and as you do
after falling 8 times
you rise 9

and she did
she moved to a mostly Black suburb
Stone Mountain

and said she was very safe
and that her neighbors called her
the White Witch

to say Naunie
was woo woo
is 49% of the truth
I called her Mother No
because if I went to her
with my current enthusiasm
she would ask me how
was I going to fund this
and what did I think
the return was going to be
Mother No
hit one home run
after another

I was one of many
to seek her counsel
my brother/friend Raven
(very woo woo)
swore by her
and pushed me
because I needed help
and I went because
he pushed me
and she charged much less
than psychotherapists
and I was broke

after the first appointment
and I think that was the one
where she taught me
"allow, accept and appreciate"

and when I would continue
to whine
she would say
"allow, allow, allow"

she would ask me
repeatedly
"What does Franklin want?"
taunting my
co-dependency
"What does Franklin want?"

Naunie helped me be more me
for she was wholly who she said she was
not an ounce of pretense or self-pity
she never retired
she probably told someone an hour before her death
"what not why, what not why, why is a lie!"
her way of saying you can feel the truth
when it is real

Naunie is still real
she cast her suffering body off
and I don't think she desires individual divinity
no cult for her
except perhaps her beloved family
Christmas is coming and Christmas
was a really big deal for Naunie

she cooked cookies and cakes
her beloved mother cooked
and made lots and lots
every year she made me an almond pound cake
it would fall and be gooey in the middle
she claimed she didn't know why
but knew I liked that part the best

I wish I had a final memory
or another one of her fiercely repetitious
admonitions
but this I can share
Naunie was eye-to-eye
whatever she said or did
she looked at me
she observed me
she showed me mercy
and in her most genuine glissade
her laughter uplifted my own
she gave me her light
to illumine my song

in memory of Naunie Batchelder

PAT

Pat was not Patricia
as she had been named
she was her father's daughter
and trained to be a dancer
against her mother's will
she was a blithe spirit
she knew how to move
wore elaborate makeup
and jewelry

there was never a brighter color
than Pat

she dismissed a Ph.D.
she was more than that
phenomenology informed her being

she gave counsel from the heart
so many were helped
and adored her
she kept her mystery close
that was her art
that was Pat
at her best

she was smart

she was radiant

she was how the heart
shines bright
in the dark of night

Pat was a star

in memory of Patricia Wren Wells

Peach Gazpacho and Peace

last night
I went with friends
to celebrate Bastille Day
at a little Alsatian restaurant
one of my favorites
near my home
it began with peach gazpacho
and ended in a caramel cream
with a heart-shaped lavender cookie
I ate every bite

I had to get up this morning
much earlier than I might
to attend continuing education
on how therapists should prepare
for death and disability
not exactly a cheery topic
but I needed the hours

this was my first in-person
professional event since the dawn
of Covid
and I was a bit leery
given the highly infectious
emergence
of a new sub-sub variant
and the reports
from numerous friends
of infection and infection

everyone wore a mask
and the air was filtered
and the presentation hit close to home

I had done some of the clean-up
when a colleague died
with no plan
how to find her clients
how to approach them
how to offer support
all ad lib
with lots of gaps
and unnecessary trauma

my friend had not prepared to die
or prepared anyone how to tell her clients
or even find them
a royal mess
a tragedy

at lunch I followed two of my colleagues
to Lucky Thai
a restaurant that no longer existed
and found them three storefronts
down the strip mall
at Cafe Bombay
where we had the buffet
and talked longer than we should
about books and politics
and encouraged each other
to continue to encourage others
to vote, to read, to connect
across the differences

on the way home
I picked up my new prescription
for my blood pressure medication
after the cortisone injection
in my knee, as predicted . . .
my blood pressure alarmed me

I called my doctor
he said double up
and my numbers are dropping

I spoke with a friend by phone
who got bad news about her eyes
and we talked at length
about how gravity, gravity, gravity
wears us down as we age
and our numbers rise
and our doctors prescribe
and we lose
our nonchalance

I will work in my garden tomorrow
and cook soup and spaghetti
and brush the cats
and my teeth
and take a nap
and release
a little bit of madness
and a little bit of sadness
in the service of relief
in the drop of my shoulders
a moment of peace

may peace spread out
over the waters
from my heart to yours
from our hearts to those hearts
who encircle ours
spread out beyond who we know
to all we know
until our peace
passes understanding

My Ordinary Life

PT Studio

I am back in Physical Therapy
my PT had Covid last week
and the week before
I was on Dad duty
in Nashville

my route is simple, short but weird
I drive down a two-lane road
to a four-way stop
and angle up through
Derrydown Way
rundown apartments
tires in yards
and then I turn into
an ultra-modern apartment complex
and my PT studio
is one of the commercial spaces
it is as surreal as it sounds

so my PT was back
a very handsome, pleasant fellow
and we went through the exercises
and I told him
these make me better
but my problem is resistant
maybe I need an MRI
it is not just muscle strength
and inflammation

he always exudes sympathy
and told me his Covid was rough
he had never been so sick

and his air conditioning at home
went out
and this is a young man
in tip-top shape
Covid isn't a joke
and I have been so lucky
and so careful
and now we have a new scare
Monkeypox
when will it ever end
in a word
never

I got donuts on the way to my chiropractor
whose 7 cats had been out of their democracy
this morning so he warned me he was running late
the donuts helped
I caught up with texts
he always pushes me in the right direction
and I was late getting home
to visit with a client on Skype
who was in remission
from his misery

after lunch and chores
the sky darkened
thunder and lightning
were much too dramatic
a torrent of rain opened
and I took a nap
with one cat on my wounded knee
and the other by my side
and the storm passed
and I had to pee
and so disrupted this hierarchy

My Ordinary Life

of lions
who only yawn and roll over
so I can feed them supper
and settle into a quiet night

I am convinced
that caring saves us
when it is back and forth
my PT and my chiropractor
the man who puts my donuts
in a small white bag
the interaction with my client
my cats who rule me
with feline determination
and the frogs and cicadas
who sing a song of forever
just above my head
much older than a human song
a lullaby
as ancient
as the Milky Way

RAIN

I backed my car
out of my garage
and the rain was falling hard
I followed the directions from my GPS
and the rain was falling hard
I got into the turn lane for the Interstate
as directed and the rain was falling hard
the Interstate was all glowing tail lights
not moving
I maneuvered over two lanes
and drove a mile to the next left turn
I pulled into a pharmacy parking lot
and called my friend Noël
I said I couldn't do the drive to Dalton
much less get through the traffic jam
to pick him up in Tucker
ever gracious he said he understood
offered to drive
and I declined
I wanted to go to this party
to celebrate the victories of two dear friends
but I am worried again about a new Covid variant
and a party before I visit my ancient father
and my own delicate nervous system
that is activated by rain, driving, glare
getting somewhere
so I texted my friends my decline
and sent lots of love
and turquoise butterflies

when I got home
I did my natural treatment

for heightened cortisol
induced by stress
I lay down on my bed
turned the heating pad
on my lower back
and massaged the ears
of my male feline
Ferdinand
until he lay down beside me
and I put my left hand
into his soft belly
and rubbed while he hugged
and purred
and we both fell asleep

love is not about another person
love is about life
breath rain belly
life

RASH

I went to the Dollar Store
for antihistamine cream
it was my first visit in almost a year
and I knew the product was cheap
what I would pay at a pharmacy or grocery
was five or six times what I paid
a dollar

every now and then my skin
breaks out
contact dermatitis is the diagnosis
but this time I don't know what
my skin has touched

the rash doesn't itch
but is not aesthetically pleasant
I don't feel pretty
I want it to go away

in the past I have had unguents
and ointments prescribed
and I still have tubes
but less toxic are the tubes
I can buy for a dollar
and apply with my fingers and a towel

I know this is stress
and my skin is my sensor
I know that I am finally feeling relief
after my last vaccination

two weeks and I can open the door to the cage
the day after tomorrow
and I am still scared to/of death
and can't quite believe in safety

my skin is talking to me
everything I held in is breaking out
my heart is still in hesitation
and won't open the door

little by little I get it
I am safer if not safe
I can break bread with my friends
in our homes

I can go forth on my myriad errands
and not fear the horsemen of the apocalypse
I won't be taken by the one called Covid
at best I can only get a runny nose

so what do I do
my body in fright
my mind moving forward
and my heart confused

baby steps, deep breaths
knowing I am safer than the world
and letting the world
catch up

my rash will go away
as it has in the past
I am not in pain
nor do I itch

my body will do its work
with a dab of medicine
and I will once again
glow from the inside out

isn't that what life
is all about?

RELATIONSHIPS

slept late
and was on my first cup of coffee
as the synchronous seminar
began on Zoom

I wasn't quite ready for the ethical intricacies
of couples counseling
but as I sipped my coffee
it began

and we learned a lot about the presenter
smart fellow with a ton of experience
I see everything from the eye of a Chinese painter
what is absent is present

we passed the day reviewing the do's and don'ts
of how to be an effective and ethical
couples therapist

our presenter said in the beginning
for those steeped in the practice
this will be an affirmation
and for all of us from newbies to oldies
we might learn a few new tricks

it was remedial for me
but I did take notes
I have done well with difficult couples
and avoided many of the pitfalls
our presenter warned us about
I know how to monitor my values
and when to offer a personal tidbit

I feel good that I have given the people
who honored me with their trust
just what they needed to get to the next
island

I am honoring the gifts of my teachers
each in radically different ways
called me out of the fog
and into the light
and onto a path
that wasn't easy
but I found a new home
nestled inside myself
who can I be other
than me

this is the point
when holding hands
joins destinies and dynasties
when a couple hires me
I think of their quandaries
and their offspring
and their ancestors
and how through
the sturm und drang
they have not let go

what we do
is who we are

Remember

what I cannot remember
doesn't usually disturb me
or bring me trouble
and yet I am reminded
I cannot remember

my brother has the proverbial
memory of an elephant
god bless him
I have forgotten large chunks
 of childhood
most of high school's angst
at least two thirds of college
and although I have a timeline
I trust more or less
if I didn't write it down
it might evaporate

I tell myself
I haven't forgotten
anything important
but how would I remember
if I have

one of my dear friends
also a therapist
says her heart remembers
and that gives me comfort

my heart remembers
the places that I played and sang
when I was too little

to be conscious of myself
my heart remembers
what foods I loved
and how my grandmothers
made them in their kitchens

my heart remembers
laughter and sorrow too
I can still laugh or cry
about something
half a century ago

and in a metaphysical moment
I can say my soul remembers
everything from my conception
to the instant of my fingers
on a keyboard typing

remember

Rest

I had to go after
half a cup of tea
for blood work
I have three or four times a year
to make sure a lizard
is not crawling up my leg
or nesting in my heart

I was on time
and chatted with a friend
in the waiting room
my doctor's office
is covered on the outside
with weather-worn Barbies

they are in the gutters
and on the window sills
my gift to him
a Thor action figure
sits in a plant
in the waiting room

in my doctor's office
the staff is either static
or ever changing
a new nurse weighed me
and sat me down
before the phlebotomist
took my blood

he was handsome too
in his black scrubs and mask

I told him I never look
and a story about being a child
afraid of needles
I hope he was amused
it didn't hurt
though I have
a junkie's arm
with bruises
black and blue

I came home
and my gardener
had cleared and mulched
he showed me his progress
he is a practical man
and decides what to do
on what makes the garden happy
he says he is not a mow and blow guy
and that is exactly why
I want him to return
in a week or when the weather
allows

I gave him the withered plant
that lost its verve and almost died
in the heat of my car

one day when he is giving a tour
of his Garden of Babylon
it will be radiant
covering a trellis with star-shaped leaves
with golden edges
and the son of his daughter
and the daughter of her son
will say

once upon a time
this was but a twig
but we have loved it
and now it is an arbor
take rest in its shade
everyone poor
everyone rich
can rest here

RESTORATION

so the wall is up and the roof is patched
the joists under the floor have been replaced and reinforced
the floor no longer squeaks when I walk past the piano
Mario and Jose Angel are off on another job
until I am back after the holiday
then they will paint and finish the floor
until then the room will be empty
of furniture and art

I am relieved to have a few days alone
before I am a week with my family
my father will have his first holiday in 71 years
without my mother
my brother and I are motherless children
she will not be present to guide or correct us
we will feel neither her love nor her critique

the cats are wondering where the furniture went
and why the wall is unpainted
and the flooring half finished
they are happy that they can roam free
though their landscape has changed

I find my work with clients twice as heavy
because of politics and the pandemic of politics
one session equals two
and if the math is right
I worked a ten-hour day

one of my best friends is in intensive care
not because of Covid
we don't know why her kidneys are failing

we don't know why her lungs are full of fluid
we don't know what to pray for
or who to pray to
or what shape mercy might take

I hear the echo of my advice
to a client in distress
open your heart and send love
into the abyss
open your heart and send love
into the void
open your heart
and love what you cannot help
but wish to avoid

open your heart
open your heart
open your heart

love what you think
you cannot love
and love more
than you think
you can

I saw the crescent moon tonight
and Venus shining so close
it made me shiver
there was no one there
but me
and still I exclaimed
oh love
oh love
oh love

ROBERT

I learned this morning
that my friend Robert died yesterday
he was taking a walk in his neighborhood
not far from my neighborhood
and collapsed on the sidewalk
he could not be resuscitated, his heart had stopped
it was the middle of the afternoon

Robert and I were friends by association
we were both a part of an existentialist
feminist spiritual community
Robert was straighter than I am gay
but he hugged with gusto
and loved across the differences

he was a pillar of our community
the tent is sagging
with his loss
his dedication
held up this little group of eccentrics
friends on the fringes
devoted to social justice
Robert was devoted
and an unlikely member

I teased him
we were both Alabama refugees
having grown up in the segregated
heart of the heart of Dixie
we shared an accent
and a sense of humor
and a knowing of how wrong

My Ordinary Life

racism can go
we were raised
in the state that elected
George Wallace
governor
where Bull Connor
sicced the dogs
and firehoses
on peaceful demonstrators
where 4 little girls
died in a church bombing
while we were both teenagers
we had a front-row seat
we knew evil was evil

Robert was the member of the board
or a committee
(he was always on one or both)
who would invite me to speak
at the First Existentialist Congregation
  of Atlanta
and often on less than desirable dates
a holiday weekend, the day after Christmas
and he knew I was likely to say yes
during Covid
he filmed me with his phone
in my garden
as an audience of one
he was the best
I could hope for or imagine
Robert was present

he was my age
and lived to see one of his fondest hopes
come true

his son married and he and his wife
had a daughter
there is a poignant photograph
of Robert holding his granddaughter
not knowing he was giving her his light
he gave his light to many
and though his light went out
it shines through hundreds of us
who Robert loved
without reserve

I can feel him
now
incandescent

in memory of Robert Stewart

Second Shot

I had done my homework and found the site yesterday
not without effort, the directions were confusing
and I was confused again today but knew I was
I made the correction quickly and arrived half an hour
before my scheduled time

it was much more impersonal than the parking lot
of the Greater Piney Woods Baptist Church
yellow tape and orange markers
this time men in Army uniforms were directing traffic
I filled out the same form
my temperature was 96.7
(proof to my conspiracy theory that my temp going
down was making a lizard out of me)
a blonde woman in a SUV broke in line in front of me
I hoped she was a surgeon getting back to the line of duty
but feared she was a politician's wife
uncharitable thoughts entered my mind
and I pushed them aside
as I inched forward remembering a slogan
on a sign in front of a church
"kindness has an echo"
efficiency made any personal connection impossible
the nurse wanted my paperwork
and came back with a syringe
this injection hurt where the one before had been painless
I parked in the designated parking area for 15 minutes
same as before, same as before I drove out symptom-free
back to the poorly-marked frontage road
and turned right onto the Buford Highway

I had promised myself I could take back roads home
the interstate was more gentle than usual
but is often full of push-and-shove trucks
and daredevil drivers
the Buford Highway is a cultural phenomenon
with restaurants and storefronts
representing myriad nationalities
I talked myself into stopping
at an international grocery store
one I often visited after dental appointments
I overcame the chorus of voices in my head
almost a year old that sang why, why, no, no
my mother told me long ago
you cannot transit life being afraid
of stepping on a snake
even though I have stepped on a snake once or twice

walking in there was a huge display of pomelos for 99 cents
I love pomelos and put one in my basket
I cruised the vegetables and herbs
getting a deal on kohlrabi
and finding some nice mint and oyster mushrooms
I found roasted tofu and rice noodles
in the kitchen section I found a device
to shred green onions
for under three dollars

everything, except the shredder, is in the fridge
my next big culinary experiment
will involve these ingredients

I did take a nap that I didn't want to wake up from

my lizard tail, a figment of my imagination
is now long enough to wrap around
the leg of another mammal
my arm seems more sore than from the first stick
but not painfully so

it took a few hours to run the gauntlet
worried at every turn if I was turning right
I am glad I stopped into the international grocery store
bought radishes and odd soft drinks
and came home and took a nap
and woke myself up for a zoom with clients

I am rambling now which is the state of my brain
once the hunter has killed, the fisherman caught
there is only the recounting and the taste of victory
only for me it is tofu and kohlrabi
tomorrow or the next day I will prepare a feast
of mushrooms, vegetables, noodles, soy sauce
with an arm that doesn't hurt
and a body that won't surrender

SHREDDING

evidently I was dealing with two different companies
that do confidential shredding right in front of you
and since I had to be compliant with all the rules of
confidentiality
I couldn't just dump a load of files at FedEx

I got a call from XXX Confidential Shredding
saying the truck would arrive at 10:30
but at 9:30 a driver from XXX Confidential Shredding
knocked at my door and I was only too happy
to cram all my client files, tax files, cancelled checks
into one big bin, he crunched it in
since it was only $75 dollars a bin

a camera inside the bin allowed me to watch
as decades of my life was shredded into confetti
and when the bin came back up and there was a handful
my driver reached deep in the bin and wadded it up
and the bin went back and the leftovers met the same fate

I told him since lockdown everything was amusing
and he said he had been working the whole time
he was a burly white guy in a surgical mask
with a tear tattooed on his cheek
and the letters in caps SATAN
in blue ink on one hand
I thought twice about giving him
my credit card number
but I did and handed him a Hamilton
lunch he exclaimed in thanks

two hours later another driver
drove up in a different-colored truck

and I apologized to him
showed him the receipt the first driver
gave me

in the still of the night
I am both unburdened of the last thirty years
and wondering why I would give SATAN
my credit card number

if you ponder a riddle
the answer is never opposite
and the truth cannot help you

tomorrow will bring a morning
unique and ubiquitous
what was will be and what will be
is always just becoming

SPLITTING THE MOON

was like walking on water
or turning water into wine
or raising dead Lazarus
a necessary miracle
for anyone who needed a sign

the sea was parted
the burning bush imparted
all we need to know
and the Virgin Mary departed
bodily into Heaven

the moon was split
the Prophet was emphatic
faith rests in art
where the eye sees twice
before it thinks
it blinks

Spider Lily Bulbs

when I went to the nursery today
I looked for the most unusual bulbs
and I asked the woman working there
why are spider lily bulbs so expensive
she stammered
and said she'd have to Google it
7 dollars for a bulb is a lot
and yet when these beauties burst forth
in September
their lacy red crowns
bring joy to my heart

I bought a cat toy at the Dollar Store
a pink fish on a string
and my cats hate it with a fervor
that brings joy to my heart
my female feline Zephyr
is the fastest being
I've ever watched
and regal Ferdinand
easily captures the pink fish
and bites it with glee

I speak on Messenger
with a dear friend who moved away
for reasons that are aligned with his destiny
I miss him and wish we were sitting across
the dinner table
he was one of the few I kept company with
when the cloud of Covid overwhelmed us
I know he is living his best life
and my heart is cheered
by a video chat

and after that
the quiet of the night
the frogs singing in the trees
the lolling of the cats
and a quiet sip of tea
lets me let go
of this mortal chain
the pain of the body
and soul
and float
free

Storyville

my life is one story built upon another
built upon my mother's stories
and my father's stories
my life is a story
built upon my grandparents' stories
my DNA

my story is in part
a Bible story
is in part
a myth from ancient Greece
a nursery rhyme
it is written in Shakespeare's hand
it is a Declaration
of Independence
of Human Rights
Leaves of Grass
a yellow brick road
a Lush Life
a Howl

my story is told upon the land
where I live
my home has been owned
since 1947 by people a lot like me
the land it was built on
was owned by some people
and worked by other people
and stolen from the first people
who wandered these woods
hunted and gathered
and before them

only deer and rabbits
and squirrels and birds
snakes and lizards
who know they are
original

trees shelter my story
the wind blows the chimes
on my porch
honeysuckle vines grow
in profusion
and the ancient frogs
sing from frost to frost

my story which began
in stardust
continues tonight
as my fingers type
and my laptop hums
and with the touch of a button
my story joins your story
and we enter eternity
together

TEA

I had tea with my friend Cal
and absorbed his holiday decor
always fabulous and sparkling
even in daylight
he said he only put out half
of everything
and that his partner Randy
lent him an artificial tree
which was very pretty
he was ambivalent
but said it was so much less work
and I remarked it smelled piney
and he pointed to a burning
pine scented candle

we at cheese and crackers
he has a marble cheese guillotine
and then chocolate covered cookies
and we drank tea
with milk and brown sugar
and caught up on who we know
and who is no more

we are both travelers
and lament that travel is so difficult
in this Covid mist
right now neither of us
will stray far from home

Cal lives in the cutest cottage ever
with the cutest garden
he has cultivated over decades

we have known each other decades longer
if we met in 1970 we have known each other
over fifty years

we won't have another fifty
we both held a moment of sorrow
for those no longer with us
over those whose accelerated aging
is a worry
and talked about the importance of naps
and a daily walk

as is tradition
I came in and left through the front door
and passed his great camellia
now in full tilt
he collected branches from the windy night
on Sunday
and I scampered across McLendon Avenue
and drove on to a final stop
before home

before Cal I had spent an hour
with my acupuncturist Faith
when we ended she asked what
was my schedule
and I said I was having tea
with a friend in the neighborhood
"perfect", she said
be gentle with yourself
"we did a lot"

well I just lay on my stomach
but I count the pins
and know she had to use extra

to balance my chi
and as there is stimulus
there is response

after I left Cal
I dropped off a holiday gift
for my friend
his neighbor Edi
and I sat on her porch
gave her tokens
received chocolate
and a loaned book
and drove home

when I arrived
I checked the mail
and did catbox duty
walked the perimeter of my garden
selected a red camellia to replace
a fallen one
and found my bed
turned on the heating pad for my back
rubbed the ears of my pal Ferdinand
and let my body relax
and float down that river
where healing happens
it was a two-cat nap
with Zephyr joining in
and we all made
amends with gravity

when I rose
the dishwasher
was ending its dirge
and I wouldn't say

that I emerged
but I peeked out
like the moon from behind a cloud
said nothing out loud
and I haven't since
I don't count talking to the cats
since they talk gibberish
and I talk nonsense
they would not understand these words
but both are curled and quiet
and the night is cold outside
and the dark has covered us
like a grandmother covers a child
with the softest blanket

TEH-LAH-NEY

with thunderstorms predicted for tomorrow
and my aging back out of whack
I conferred with my traveling companion
and we agreed to leave early

I backed into a rut
that we could not push our way out of
our good fortune, Tuscumbia's Fire Chief
lived next door to our rental
heave ho and he and Roger pushed
my car out of the rut and onto
the grassy alleyway
and we escaped

a really glamorous young woman
an intern from the University of North Alabama
was our guide at Fame Studios
we got to come within breathing distance
of the piano that Aretha played
on Ain't Never Loved a Man . . .
and the Hammond organ played by Gregg Allman
and the baby grand played recently by Alicia Keys

we drove across north Alabama to just above Cullman
where my father's parents grew up
I resisted taking Roger to the ultra kitschy
Ave Maria Grotto
we were both physically and emotionally exhausted
from visits and visitations

after time with our lifetime friends and their nine dogs
and two parrots outside of Hohenwald, Tennessee

we drove down the Natchez Trace Parkway
to mile marker 339 and made a left

Tom's Wall contains what seems a million stones
one man and his son lifted over thirty years
to build a sanctuary in honor of
his great, great grandmother
who had walked the Trail of Tears
and walked back so she could hear the river singing
the Tennessee at Muscle Shoals

Tom created a magic circle and two promenades
you can't take your cell phone inside the magic circle
explained his son
the fairies don't like it

as I walked to and fro
in and out of sacred space
the first and only living memorial
the son said to a Native American woman
I felt the cool of the stones
and looked into their faces
I felt the trees that overarched
and then when my mind relaxed
I saw the faces in the shadows
of the dappled light
they were winking at me
they were whispering in a language
I knew but didn't know

our next stop in Florence, Alabama
was the Rosenbaum House
designed by Frank Lloyd Wright
a work of genius
negotiated between the architect

and the occupants
and the landscape it sits upon

first occupied in 1940 as a wedding present
from Stanley Rosenbaum's father to Stanley
and his new wife Mildred, the couple
argued with Wright over having windows
with screens, this before air conditioning
Wright compromised, the screens would be brass
and shimmer in the sunlight

in many ways the house feels like a stationary train
narrow halls, a galley kitchen
every space used
a perfect example of Wright's Usonian philosophy
to make elegant, efficient and affordable homes
the Rosenbaums lived there for almost fifty years
raised four sons and sat tight
as the house slowly deteriorated
the house and their belongings were donated to the city
and two years later had been restored
what was once a home became a shrine

it is another world of paneled walls and ceilings
Wright always thinking of the play of light
once on a hundred acres, now on ten
a Japanese garden represents outer space
and a Wright-designed angel guards the door

we visited another house in nearby Tuscumbia
it was the childhood home of Helen Keller
replete with the well where Annie Sullivan
taught her finger spelling and she
learned her first word, one hand under
the steam from the well wet
and the other spelling water

there was the formal dining room
where the famous food fight between her and Annie
resulted in her defeat
Helen was an imp and delighted in locking her mother
in the food pantry and Annie in her upstairs bedroom

Annie took her up north to schools specialized in training
deaf and blind persons to get along better in society
Helen decided she wanted to speak and spent hours
feeling Annie's throat as she talked, sticking her fingers
in Annie's mouth so she could learn
how to move her tongue

the hard work paid off, she attended Radcliffe College
graduated cum laude and set out on a career to help
raise awareness of the challenges and possibilities for blind
and disabled people
she also raised her voice for social justice and civil rights

she traveled the world, met eminent figures
like Rabindranath Tagore
and every US President from Hoover to Kennedy

in the back of the cottage beyond the tributes from
international Lions Clubs is a pine tree planted
from a pine seed taken to the moon
thirty feet high and there is nothing
obviously special about it
I did bend down and slipped a pinecone that had fallen
from its branches into my pocket

I left it in the car last night for no particular reason
maybe I was just tired. I had spent the previous week
looking in on my 93-year old father and my brother's dog
Barkley. It was simple enough to visit with dad, talk with
his caregiver, let Barkley out, rub his belly.

I thought a visit with friends and then some sightseeing
might create balance but I was right for the wrong reasons
my family week was leitmotif
visiting the Rosenbaums, Helen Keller, singer-songwriter
heaven and a ceremonial spot honoring Tey-la-nay who
had walked the Trail of Tears in reverse to find a singing
river rearranged my molecules

we are all listening as we walk
we are all listening as we talk
we are all looking for the word for water
for the place of balance
where the soul can fly
we are all walking down a sacred avenue
saluting each other as pass we do
we cannot help ourselves
or help each other
we can build lives
of beauty
we can learn to speak in tongues
we can go back
when compelled
to where we come from
like Teh-la-nay

THANK YOU KINDLY

I like the cornbread
at Cracker Barrel
and the greens and beans
full of country ham

I am glad I can now sit down
in their corny country dining room
and drink ice tea
and put pepper sauce
raw onion and chow chow relish
on my food

I always want to buy something tacky
in the gift shop lobby
but have refrained
for over twenty years
the plastic parrot that parrots
what you say
a Cracker Barrel trophy
still sits on my piano

I did not buy the frog
that charms with sparkling solar bubbles
or the sundress
covered with pretty turtles

I wore my mask
coming in and going out
the waitresses did too
but most of the customers
in rural north Georgia
near Dalton

did not play
by the rules

the rules say
I can take off my mask
when I sit down at my table
but put it back on
if I have to use the restroom
or wander in the gift shop

as my friend Roger waited
to pay our bill
I sat outside
beside a large Latinx
family
celebrating the graduation
of a daughter
who was wearing
 her red mortarboard hat

they seemed jubilant
some masked
some half masked
and their heroine
breathing freely

we filled up with gas
at the service station next door
and drove on

one more stop at a rest station
atop Monteagle Mountain
I called my father
Roger called our friend Robin
(logistics)

and I donned my mask
to enter the restroom
no one else but me
 was masked inside the restroom

as I exited the building
I held the door for the man behind me
a six-foot-plus bearded trucker
who was maskless
who said
thank you kindly

THAT STUBBORN TOOTH

that stubborn tooth
that had rested in the back of my lower jaw
for sixty-five years
did not want to come out

it was cracked and couldn't be crowned
I put off the extraction for over a year
Covid was my cover plus it didn't hurt
about a month ago it began
to tell me

time was growing nigh
something cold or something hot
something sweet or spicy
anything like wine or vinegar
made the volcano rumble

sometimes the displeasure was brief
and sometimes it dogged my sleep
and I offered ibuprofen to the angry god
and it relented less
and sent more grief

when the pain finally got the best of me
my dentist, his clientele now vaccinated
had no appointments for a week
I could come as a walk-in and wait
but I didn't take the bait

the last extraction had been awful
I had been unprepared for a broken tooth
with a dangling root

and he had done three extractions
for the price of one

it took six hours for the pain
to be undone
and a sleepless night
and a restless day
I had to pay

this time I said numb me up
numb me up and numb me up
and he did and he did and he did
and I left feeling no pain
but the drain was deep

my stubborn tooth had to be taken
like Gaul in three parts
there was great push and pull
leverage and brute force
before the crater could be packed

I came home with bloody gauze
in my mouth
and the three pieces of the tooth
in an envelope to join
my tooth necropolis

I did not take the pain medication
before the numbness wore off
and fell into a trough of hurt
and fog and felt afraid
to eat or walk

to ease the pain
I sacrificed the night

I was drifting on a life raft
and waiting for the light
when I slept a few hours

until day called me to stand upright
and I did and did my duties
until I struggled through another night
trading waking up for ibuprofen
and ibuprofen and ibuprofen

I am grateful for the medicines
that kill the pain and run away infections
I am grateful that my dentist
is so skillful that I suffered no more
than I had to

I am grateful for that molar that ground up
the gristle of life, the nuts and the roots
and gave a good fight
and I hope tomorrow
my jaw will relax

my memory will fade
and the battle will subside
no more ache
no more pain
what was lost

is now a gain

THE BODY I DANCE IN

the accident was my fault
I was doing repetitive exercises
mindlessly
I mean how much thought is needed
if I am repeating a simple motion
30 times
I can barely pay attention
enough to count

and that worked for seventy years
I rarely hurt myself
I moved slowly enough
I did not overexert
but I did not have to think

I am lying face down
with acupuncture needles
in my lower back
and much to my surprise
part of letting go
comes as grief

pain is ebbing
tension is subsiding
and I am crying
for nothing and for something
I am not so elastic
so resilient
and I can't be cavalier
or casual
I must cultivate
a new grace

dance much more
deliberately

and when I get up
from the table
my circuits humming
my body quiet
I walk out to my car
open the door
and get in
with different
choreography

I have not given up
the dance
but sharpened
and honed
and honored
the body
I dance in

THE FROGS ARE SINGING

the frogs are still singing tonight
as if nothing has happened
since last summer
or the summer a hundred years ago
or the summer a hundred thousand years ago

their symphony is not simple
listen closely
there is not a note of repetition
everything is included
the airplane that flies above
the siren on the avenue
the bark of a dog

and yet the chorus is consistent
the conductor has never appeared
the song is the long song of creation
if one tree falls then another grows up
if there is a storm there is also calm

I am caught up in my personal turmoil
the heat is on with elections and a plague
my personal grief, my sorrows
the frogs keep singing
their wages never change
they do not go on strike
but always get renewal
they care little for politics
and less for my anxieties

on the porch my cats are at rest
the night is resonant but not unusual

the soundtrack of the frogs singing
they have known since they were kittens
I hear the same song
it slowly envelopes me
and except for the faraway siren
and the next plane flying over
except for my neighbor's dogs barking
like all dogs who do their job
I hear the same song
the frogs are singing
the frogs are singing

the frogs are singing

THE HOURS

why else do we struggle to go on living, no matter how
compromised, no matter how harmed?
　　　　– Virginia Woolf

a rough day is when the demons
win 13 to 11
points are points
gravity is a factor
tragedy is more Chopin
and less Cabaret

after 70
the odds change
and 13 is more common than 11
though once 11 was unusual
and even 9
was uncomfortable
mostly the odds
subtracting heartbreak
were under 7
under 5
a cold was 3
a restless night
a 2

the worst thing I know
from having longevity
in my genes
is 13 will quickly become 14
and before I have time
to write my memoir
19

and as I watch the sun setting
surrounded by comfort and compassion
my 23 will dip slowly
into the perfect ocean
and my 24 will glow
with love

The News Is Often Unbearable

mass shootings
senseless wars
wildfires and floods
the politics of brutality

I sit in a neighborhood
Italian-style restaurant
lots of pasta on the menu
gelato next door
but no Italians
it is a breezy night
after a rain
and I sit at the end of the table
my two friends facing each other
they have known each other for decades
one is from India
the other from Pakistan
and we avoid politics as long as we can
and then I listen
so I can understand
how personal politics can be
my Indian friend explaining
my Pakistani friend inquiring
and I am ordering our dessert
pistachio gelato
and lemon sorbet
two flavors that could not be
more different
melting beside each other
in the bowl

our three spoons scooping
stories not jibing
history in fragments
friendship walking on glass
who broke the window
I don't know
and the three of us
all post-colonials
finish dessert
and go to our cars
that are parked in direct
opposition
I back out with my Indian friend in tow
my Pakistani friend is free to drive forward
we follow her out
into the same cool night
going home
to seperate places
each with a tiffin of pasta
we can warm tomorrow
and remember
how we sat together
with our different stories
and ate our dinner
in peace

THE NEXT BREATH

I'm turning my love-life over to God
I am giving him-her-them the keys to my car
I am trusting that the thunderstorms
of my destiny
are what come before the rainbows

I don't have an image or creed or idol
to bow before or behave before
but I put my best foot forward
I push my toes down into the ground
and my raise my hands to heaven

I believe in the Resonance
between my good will
and Grace

and I absolve myself
of sin in every trace

my history informs my destiny
and it is crooked and craggy
and locked in mystery

I can only take the next breath
I can only take the next breath
I can only, only, only
take the next breath

THE SONG OF
THE CLEAN PLATE

I fed my father, 94, supper
I did not grow and wash and simmer
the turnip greens
like his parents did
I did not scrape the corn cob
after cutting the corn
I did not shell
the beans
and the cornbread
was from a mix

they did not catch the fish
tilapia is not white trout
hooked in the river
there was no cornmeal
in the pantry so I cooked the fish
coated in Bisquick

I put leftover bacon
in the greens
butter in the butter beans
the creamed corn from a can
was a mess but yielded
a few good spoons

I didn't say to my father
whose memory
is a sieve
that this is what your mother cooked
this is what you would wish for

if you could, your last meal
on execution row

we were almost silent
during dinner

and he cleaned his plate

THE STATE OF THINGS

I read about the ice shelves of Antarctica collapsing
and the water rising all around the world
tornadoes erase civilization
along a two-hundred-mile track in Kentucky
and a new variant of the Covid virus
shuts down the Netherlands

Senate recalcitrance
keeps social progress at bay
racism denies that it exists
lgbtq refugees huddle
in a camp in Kenya
hungry, brutalized
no doctors
no way out

tyrants strut across the world stage
as if it was 1932
and if that isn't enough
people are so ignorant and frightened
they will believe anything is true

I don't know how to solve this riddle
it is bigger than my brain
and deeper than my heart
but I know that where I am
is where I start

who needs a phone call
who needs a visit
who needs a pot of soup
a loaf of bread

who needs a hug
who needs an arm around their shoulder
who needs a dollar or two
who needs a welcome
hey come over to my house
let me feed you supper
let me listen to your story
let me hire your son or daughter

I have so little and so much
less money and more touch
less to legislate
and more to compensate
I am not a crane
I cannot bear the strain of tons
but maybe in a moment
when you need a little lift
my love
is leverage enough

THE TWO SIDES
OF MY BRAIN CONVERSE

I tell myself
call a friend
I ask myself
what is the next
right thing to do
these instructions
irritate my
inner philosopher
who demands
introspection
insight
meaning

the old woman
who lives in the back
of my soul
is far more direct
clean the stove
brush your teeth
call Kevin
she's the one
who feeds the cats
and tells me
make a sandwich

my philosopher
wants lofty answers
to lofty questions
when did time begin
and when will it end
and begin again

I like to follow his line
of reasoning
and I want to know
how much mystery
is yet to be fathomed

the old woman says
to catch a fish
bait a hook
sit by a river
and wait
let your hands listen
and maybe the fish
will get unlucky

she smiles
she knows how to fry a fish
my philosopher
is still looking for the exact
temperature to the nanosecond
when water comes to a boil
he will wait eternity
for his tea

The Truth
Will Make You Odd

"The truth will make you odd"

avatar Flannery O'Connor

may have said these words

meant these words

she certainly knew these words

and typed them onto white paper
on a typewriter
in her writing/living/sleeping room
at Andalusia, her family farm
just outside of Milledgeville
where half the population
lived in a state institution
for the unstable, criminally insane
mentally challenged, outrageous
and subversive elements
they grew their own food
and competed with the prisons
to manufacture license plates
for vehicles
and boats

a license
to fish
to carry a gun
to get married

to bury
or fix hair
a license
to be a dentist
or a doctor
or a chiropractor
or a fortune teller
oh, oh that there were
a license
to die

put it in the aviation column
a license to fly a drone
a helicopter
a jet plane
a license to say no more
I am worn
and I am weary
a license to fly away

oh Lord

I have been spending my worry
on my father
he is never at peace
nothing that will kill him
but it is like a thousand
paper cuts

my brother and I understand
my brother's wife and sons
understand
and I understand
my father's doctor
understands

his caregiver
absolutely
understands

but he is gaining weight
does that mean he is gaining strength
it has only been a year
since his wife of over seventy
years
died beside him

he is blind in his grief
he cannot hear himself
speaking

he can't remember
his anger
that pops like popcorn

he can't unsay
nor can we be
in disagreement

my father and I
still face the same dilemmas
when to go to sleep
and when to wake up
my female feline Zephyr
gives me three chances
three chances to arise
soon after the sun rises

when you approach a loss
think of it as a tunnel
sometimes it is a long, long tunnel

sometimes a tunnel is brief
and you pass through

in between the ambient light
and the tunnel
something falls away
we lose appetite
thirst
and we wait
for the slow, slow
beat of the heart
to stop

THE WEATHER
CAN CHANGE QUICKLY

after I said goodbye to my host
and my co-celebrants
walked down three flights of stairs
gingerly
and drove out of the labyrinth
of the complex where I shared
an evening of delight
good food, good wine, good conversation
I had not gotten a mile down the road
before the bottom dropped out
and the rainfall so intense the road
was flooding
and visibility was sketchy
and my heart was pounding
it had been not so long ago
when I was almost swept away
in a flood

after dinner my friend Paul P
had given us all dream stones
given to him by a Toltec shaman
on a recent trip to Mexico
it was in my breast pocket with my mask
and I touched the stone
and chanted get me home
get me home
get me home safe
and maybe it was spirit
maybe it was skill
maybe it was luck
but it got me home

got me home
got me home
safe

I can feel stress fading
cortisol levels dropping
distraction helping
my body deflating
more than two hours later
with lots of distractions
I can feel my breath
slow and gentle
I can know that I am safe
it is this simple
like Noah I survived
the flood of feelings
and rain making rivers out of roads
the storm has subsided
or moved on
and the frogs are singing
and telling me
dear human
take another deep breath
deep breaths are free
have as many as you need
let your shoulders drop
stretch your jaw out of clench
and another deep breath
the night is quiet
our song is like the Milky Way
we sing what we see
and be what we be
go to sleep sweet prince
you are safe
you are sound
you are free

THERE MUST BE
A SHELTERING PLACE

there must be a sheltering place
for weary souls
there must be a river that sings life
back to bones
there must be a waterfall
that splashes the body
there must be a rainbow
when the sun crosses
the mist

I am a rainbow
I am a waterfall
I am a river
I am a sheltering place

I am a rainbow
I am a waterfall
I am a river
I am a sheltering place

no one can hear me
no one can see me
nobody knows
that I am here

no one can hear me
no one can see me
nobody knows
that I am here

I am a rainbow
I am a waterfall
I am a river
I am a sheltering place

no one can see me
no one can hear me
no one can wipe
the tears from my face

I am a rainbow
I am a waterfall
I am a river
I am a sheltering place

THEY ARE COMING

in the morning
I have to be ready from 8 until 2
so maybe in the early afternoon
but after 8 and before 2
they are coming

everything is labeled
boxes 1-12
each with a printed label
ready to be taken

tonight I will light incense
and ring bells
tonight I will talk with Lord Ganesh
who overcomes all obstacles

somehow these twelve boxes
each holding a hundred books or more
that spell the history of my hopes and desires
that hold in their covers particles of my
 imagination

they will be picked up box by box
put in a truck and taken to another truck
taken to a warehouse
outside of Chicago to be wrapped and weighed

how will they make their journey
from Chicago to Mumbai
will they float up and out of the Great Lakes
or be trucked to New York or Boston

when will the great ship take them
over the icy Atlantic
down through the Mediterranean Sea
to the throat of Egypt

will they float through
the Suez Canal
and down the Red Sea
and round the Horn of Africa

will they sail the Arabian Sea
past pirates and gunboats
and float down the Indian coast
to the port of Mumbai

will they make it there in time
to avoid the monsoons
will they be carried on trucks
to Thane and the college library

I have marked down the building
and the floor and given them
the numbers to call
these books have been long anticipated

I am sure they seem ephemeral
I promised them two and a half years ago
then the pandemic jammed up shipping
and receiving

I will be waiting
hoping that half a ton of books*

a thousand books
sent at the end of an American winter

will climb up the stairs
and sit waiting to be unpacked
book by book
in an Indian summer

and by this time in a year
be in the eyes and hands
and hearts
of a thousand Indian students

*The books made their journey safely from my home in Atlanta,
carried most of the way on the container ship Ivanhoe and are now in
the library of Joshi Bedeker College in Thane, Maharashtra, India.

TO MASK OR NOT TO MASK

it seems it has become
a perpetual question
when I met my friends
at Athens Pizza
one was masked
and the other not
I did not wear a mask
when I entered
it is a spacious restaurant
and my friends were seated
in an empty section

our waitress was not masked
and of course we ate our pita
and hummus our pizza and gyro
without
we drank our water with lemon
and talked about past and future
adventures
and the virulent
new variants
and did not mention
our individual differences
I paid for our lunch
my birthday treat
handing money
under a plexiglass screen
to a cashier
who wasn't masked
and when we hugged
in the parking lot
I was still unmasked

My Ordinary Life

and one friend was
and the other wasn't
and as I drove to the gas station
to fill up my tank
(not yet $90 dollars)
I wondered if I felt
a tinge of regret
but I am fine
as far as I can define
and the frogs in my forest
are singing in all keys
and my cats are in slow mo
and the news
well no, no, no

my lungs are clear
and my voice is bright
and my aches and pains
will yield to the night
and I will find my way
through sleep to the light
of tomorrow

VULNERABILITY

I am sitting with four of my closest women friends
in my friend Rae Lynne's kitchen
we are eating strawberries and pineapple
and vegetable crudites and putting hummus
on gluten-free crackers
the table is arrayed with pottery from LaDonna
a gift from her and her potter/lawyer husband
and we are talking about pain

if I could guess I was a 2
and Jill was a 3
and LaDonna was a 6
and Emily and Rae Lynne
each a 7
we all explained and empathized
we talked about trauma and pain
the parts that hurt
healing and how we heal
and alluded to the fear
age will eclipse healing

we ate fruit and nuts
and at the end we ate
a gluten free chocolate torte
that tasted like a candy bar
and sang happy birthday to each other

we talked about the two of us who were missing
Pat and Barb died much too young
when Covid had us all locked down
Pat in her early sixties
Barb in her early seventies

gone too soon
like drowning victims
whose hands we could
not hold
whose lives we could not save
who we lost to the currents
that might have taken us too

Jill said softly
maybe it was them who let go
maybe it was their turn
maybe it was something
we could not fathom
maybe I will be next
or you will be next
but next will proceed
another next
until there is a last

Emily had brought a box
of trinkets from Pat's office
I selected a stone orb
and a metal bird that will house
a candle
I took half a dozen pieces
of the pottery LaDonna
gave us
mugs and tiny vases
secured in a box
of colored tissues

Emily drove me home
in her little yellow car
down the Stone Mountain Freeway
she said she was driving

like a race-car driver
but I was unafraid
she has the skill

and I full of gluten-free
chocolate torte
with a box full of ceramics
and tchotchkes in the backseat
had no fear

we are all headed in the same direction
some of us will get there first
and some of us will be later than sooner
but I know in the end
there will be cake and strawberries
and stories about what had happened
and we will laugh and sigh
and hold our breaths
until the last of us finishes the race
and joins the rest of us
in a party that will never end

WAITING FOR THE CAKE

my friend is turning 65
and her husband contrived a surprise
she knew there was a little party
but did not know the guest list
our mutual friend and my neighbor
Emily and I drove out into suburbia
my friend was indeed surprised
and it was nice to celebrate
with her family and friends
Emily said as we walked up the steps
let's not stay too long
and I agreed
she has pain from ailments
and my knee hurts
and I am socially exhausted
from a week of caregiving
with my father
in Nashville
I told her we had to stay for the cake
and we did
and it was worth the wait
worth singing happy birthday
to dear Jill now eligible for Medicare
who fanned out the candle flames
with a napkin
no blowing out candles
in times of Covid
and we ate the cake, delicious
gluten-free with raspberry sauce
and limped out of the lovely home
of our hosts and drove back
to our lovely homes before dark

and we talked about wounded knees
and aching backs and how to lend support
as these problems become facts
Emily said, nothing hurt before I turned 70
and, alas, I know it is so
you can't expect an old lawnmower
to run smoothly
and I wonder
do machines feel pain
do they ache and throb
do they need lubrication
like the Tin Man?

and if this is so
where is my oil can?

WE DIDN'T TALK ABOUT THE WEATHER

we didn't talk about the weather

we talked about our families
we talked about our travels
we talked about construction projects
and the mayhem of electricity
and festivals coming again
we talked about the passing of friends
and once we had all talked
we took two minutes of quiet
to count our blessings
here we were in a circle of 8
here we were with friendships
adding up to over a century
here we were some veterans of Viet Nam
all of us survivors of two pandemics
Marvin, our gentle facilitator
had asked me to say something
when the silence ended
and I said I was thankful
for the years of friendship
in our circle
and that we lived in peace
and plenty
and wished the same
for everyone
everywhere
and then we took our plates
from Floyd's lovely table
and ate the food we all

brought to share
and after cake there were hugs
and a decision when to meet again
and on the drive home
thankfully to the East
as the sun was setting in the West
I was full on many levels
most of all
full of love

We Couldn't Escape The Joy

we had a lovely dinner
neither of us could finish
and drove home with the other half
in a cardboard box
we were talking about friends
expressing concerns
and our conversation had turned to cults
we are both unsuitable for cults
we are square pegs in the round holes
of cults
and suddenly we saw in the sky above
a double rainbow
and gasped and sighed
and said no more of cults
but drank in the beauty

the rainbows shifted
they should have been left
but over the next hillock
they were right
we couldn't track them
they were always opposite
and seemed to disappear
only to grow stronger
and we laughed
at this unexpected blessing

Kamla had been beset by worries
and I had too
we are both growing older
and uncertainty is in our shadow
what is around the corner

a common lament
and this time
our questions were answered
rainbows
rainbows
radiant rainbows
we couldn't escape
the joy

You Bless Our Future

refugee

how to flee

first question
how deep is the sea
how wide is the land
can we withstand

second question
floating in uncertainty
will I be allowed
or returned?

third question
should I relent
or persist

if I am where I have chosen to be
if I have fled my homeland
if I have taken my children
and elders on a long march
from home to the sea

and if we have been given life jackets
(more life expectancy than what we had . . .
and we were hungry and thirsty
and holding on to each other
and we know a sister was about to give birth
and then they stole the motor from our boat
and pushed us back with their oars

and we languished
in the unforgiving sea)

we did not stop
loving each other
we gave each other breath

how many days did we love each other
into life
how did we learn that famished hands
exhausted hands, old hands and children's hands
hold hold hold
and we held on

for us
and for you born here now anew
we knew you were coming
we knew we were bringing you
to peace and plenty

you bless our future
our future
you bless

our future

You Never Know

I had the MRI on Tuesday
and imagined I was in 2001 Space Odyssey
all the weird sounds and bleeps
as this amazing machine
looks inside my knee

I had my second Monkeypox vaccination yesterday
it was more expedited than the first
I was in and out in a short time
and my public health nurse
a tall woman with a Caribbean accent
held my arm with her plastic glove
as she gave me a subcutaneous injection
and spoke to me in dulcet tones
about how to take care
of what was a pinch
and now is a spider bite

I saw clients
and cooked dinner
for my dear friend Kilian
he is leaving for Qatar
next week
and we haven't visited in a month
and so we savored every morsel
and every syllable

this morning I saw Dr. Cruz
my knee doc for the results
my MRI could spy
that my x-ray couldn't see
more arthritis inside my knee

and some torn cartilage
she asked does it hurt
and no, it doesn't
and doesn't keep me up
at night
she said you might not want
to run a marathon
and I smiled
I don't run unless I'm chased
I do have resentment
having avoided sports
my whole life long
I have the injury
of an athlete
but I know, I know
what has gone wrong

tonight my friend Cary
was reading from his new novel
at my favorite bookstore
Charis, just around the corner
and my friend Craig
was his interlocutor
Cary is a true New Yorker
his style is bold
and his book is brilliant
Craig asked all the right questions
and we got to peer
through the mirror of time
when truth was breath by breath
and survival was a wonder

you never know
when your number is up
like in my generation

the draft boards held a lottery
if you live in Russia today
your number is up
if you live in . . .
your number is up
if you live in an aging body
your number can be pulled
so you put in earplugs
pretend the clarion call
is a leaf blower
make a cocktail of denial
with a twist
straight up

so I know my knee is okay
no tumor or other horror
just a function of my age
and I know my smallpox vaccination
that left a scar on my six-year-old arm
has been updated
and I know I have brilliant friends
who are celebrated

but I will never know
never know
what I will never know
until I do

ZIKR

my dream life is a labyrinth
I think Carl Jung would agree
and if I had been writing down my dreams
all poems are dreams, dreams for fifty years
you might think I would have met my Minotaur
or found my damn way out

neither has been the case
I do not know where or what I will lose tonight
last night I couldn't read the number on my dorm key
which took me hither and thither
through cafes and bookstores
and finally I distracted a kindly matron
who turned the fob over in my hand
it all made sense
and when I found my room
I woke up

having an extensive imagination
augmented by lots of novels and movies
I will come up with something else tonight
it could be a forest or a parking lot
or winding city streets
and I know the Minotaur is me
and he will no more catch me
than I will confront him
because then, game over
we will both die
in each other's arms

Postscript

everyday I live my ordinary life so lovely so rich and so sweet it doesn't seem to matter how it repeats itself over and over goes round and round where its been to where its going everyday I live my ordinary life so lovely so rich and so sweet it doesn't seem to matter how it repeats itself over and over goes round and round where its been to where its going everyday I live my ordinary life so lovely so rich and so sweet it doesn't seem to matter how it repeats itself over and over goes round and round where its been to where its going everyday I live my ordinary life so lovely so rich and so sweet it doesn't seem to matter how it repeats itself over and over goes round and round where its been to where its going everyday

THE ACHE IS GONE

the inner chamber of my right knee
had been hollowed out by the twin djinns
of fear and grief
they were living there
intertwined like yin and yang
and their discourse
was all in the red of pain

Dr. Singh opened the chamber
and cleaned it out
he said the bones were still good
but the cartilage had been devoured
he put in plastic to mediate
and soften
and robbed the djinns of their den

now there is tenderness
bruising, swelling
the pain comes from healing
and my whole body feels it
even more my spirit
so intertwined with grief and fear
has ceased its spinning dreams
and though my feet are still learning
to dance the old steps
I am steady as I go
and hope has started
calling again

Vax 5

I made an appointment online
at the closest site I could find
and the next day I was in line
and didn't have to wait too long
the pharmacist told me not to stray
and I didn't go too far
just down cosmetics
and up through cheese
when I hear my name called
you can sit behind the partition
and I did
a young African American woman
had my syringe in a plastic bag
on a tray
and before I could say
what are the side effects
I was duly injected
and she said a sore arm
flu-like symptoms
(take a tylenol and ibuprofen)
and anxiety
the last one had an echo

I had a fancy dinner with old friends
and a cocktail and a little wine
and I was fine
until three in the morning
and I felt flu-like symptoms
and took an ibuprofen and a tylenol
and cuddled with my cats
back in bed with a little dread
and when anxiety got tired of me

slept sweetly
and had no symptoms
when my zen alarm
toned three tones

I had to read poetry
you see, in India
at 9:30
and have coffee
and vaccine-reward donuts
and finish my taxes
and at the very last moment
chose three poems to read
all about vulnerability
one was me and my friends
chirping away about our frayed lives
another about my ancient father
wandering, stumbling through his fog
and another about a dear friend and I
losing our train of serious conversation
because double rainbows adorned the sky
had followed us
all the way home

I listened to five excellent poets
only one in my time zone
and then worked with my gardener
to finish with my garden duties
and finally fix my taxes
and meet friends for a ramble
in another enchanted garden
full of fairies
and come home to tumble
into a nap

I tidy up
help a friend with her vaccine appointment
we have dinner al fresco
and as the season has changed
when the light goes
the chill comes
and I drive her home

my cats are waiting for me
wanting to be brushed
and praised
and I do
before a dip into the news
chilly too
I can't stay long
before I towel up
and stretch my vocal chords
so I can sing you this song
don't hold your breath
life is well past
anything but magic
don't plant your feet
admit defeat
life is well past
anything but magic
being right
being wrong
is the same song
in a different key
life is well past
anything but magic
anything but magic
anything but magic

HOW LONG DO YOU GRIEVE YOUR ANCESTORS?

last week was the 4th anniversary
of my mother's death
and the first birthday after
my father's death
isn't grief
just the frozen fear
of death

my ancestors
the ones I know about
lived longer than most
this was not valor
but genes
and luck

my mother was lucky
and unlucky
her aunts lived past her
into their late 90's
her arthritis
was persistent pain
Covid gave her an exit
she refused to go to a hospital
the stomach virus, not Covid
weakened her
no appetite
no swallowing
she drifted on a float
in the pool of her dreams

her only regret was leaving us
with our father
she had hidden his dementia
she kept saying, I'm sorry
we didn't understand
until she was gone
our father died
more economically
he was a practical man
and once he could
no longer be himself
he made his last
executive decision
and let go

do I miss old people
suffering
I do not
do I take wreaths to graves
I do not
do I weep without reason
I do
do I rock myself to sleep
I rock myself to sleep

sometimes
I feel a wave of grief
and I cry for whom
I do not know
it might be
just a sob
or maybe
I let go
a lamentation

this is just history
repeating history
no matter the ceremony
the monument
the drama

you grieve
just as you breathe
call it a cult
say it is ritual
somewhere in your heart
you cry
for a grandmother
a lover
a best friend
another older relative
who dies and leaves
another hole
in the wall
death penetrates
and somehow finds you
always alone
and sometimes
welcoming
open heart
open arms
ancestor to ancestor
open soul

ONE OF THOSE PLACES

my father should no longer be living alone
everyone but him agrees
he says he is NOT NOT NOT
going to that place
and all my efforts to muster alliance
and get him to the tipping point
have failed
I tell him
you don't have to
until you have to
and we change the subject
he has things to do
but admits he can't do them
he wants to go outside
but fear of falling
holds him in
and I agree
now is not the time
in the summer heat
to fall outside
we agree
to stay cool

a week later
I am awake and cannot find
succor in sleep
and I am thinking
of my next visit
while his caretaker
spends a week with her grandkids
at the beach
and I am glad

not to go
but that I can go
I can be in his habitat
with him
and his history

I remember when his mother
was moved to one of those places
and I drove to Birmingham
to pick through her artifacts
and the sadness I felt
driving away with pottery
and silverware
that I could never return
there was no there there
she was gone
disappearing into
one of those places

so this time if he is still in place
may be the last time
and when he has disappeared
into one of those places
I will never sleep under my parents' roof
eat at their table
be a child in their home
ever again
amen

AND HE DID

grace is snowfall
no exit for days
when my brother can visit
my father has been in bed
not eating
the staff at assisted living
says hospice
but the doctor doesn't visit
until Thursday

the next day my brother visits
Dad is still in bed
not eating but can squeeze his hand
yes or no
I know
I think days ahead
and plan my journey

my brother visits the next day
no squeeze of the hand
no communication
he tells me
I think Dad will last for days
and I plan my journey
nothing wrong with his heart
or lungs or kidneys

the day after
my brother visits
no response

Dad is in deep sleep
and dies in the afternoon
no pain, no surprises

ten days before he died
we talked on the phone
he predicted his departure
and I said
Dad, if the bus comes
get on the bus
if the bus comes
get on the bus

and he did

REVEILLE

aperture
an opening
a camera setting
how close
how far
how bright
how dark

I am sitting in the memorial garden
between the sanctuary
and the fellowship hall
there is a fountain
and memorial bricks
dedicated to past and future
generations
it is sunny but a little cold
the bench has a cushion
but I still feel the bench

I am waiting for my brother
and sister-in-law to exit
choir practice
and follow them
into the sanctuary
it is so so Christian

prayers, scripture
all references
this is what Christians do
no different from Muslims
or Jews or Jains or Hindus
an incantation

of the familiar
the rites, the bones
of the fairy tale

and my bones
are pushing back
I will not recite
the Lord's Prayer
or the Nicene Creed
the words of the hymns
catch in my throat
the minister's message
is lost on me
I don't believe

I am relieved
with the last Amen
wait for the reception
for my late father and my mother
generously provided
by the members of the church
I am given bread and jam
for being a new
attendee
I will consume
I do not believe
that Christian jelly
will reconvert me
I am lost
not so much a sinner
but lost to the faith
to the fairy tale
I believe in bread

later in front of my father's church
the same prayers
the same scripture
the placing of his stainless-steel cylinder
next to my mother's in the columbarium
my brother's friend playing bagpipes
as he had for my mother
brings tears

I am sitting alone
no father, no mother
that alone
new to me at 73
that alone

the pastor mumbles the final words
scripture or prayer
who cares?
the piper pipes
Amazing Grace
and feelings rise up
I could cry if I had a shoulder
my nephews and their wives
offer solid hugs
the pastor offers me
my father's flag
he was a veteran
I did not expect this
I am the oldest son
the one who
fills in at the top
of the hierarchy
the one who sat alone
at seventy-three
finally an orphan

looking out at history
disappearing
I am the next in line
and I am
the end
of time
a flag
in my lap
reveille

WE WILL ALWAYS
LOVE EACH OTHER

I have written about the deaths of my parents
and the constrictions of Covid
and my knee failing me not once
but twice
I have written about the weather
about friendship
about the loss of friends
about growing older
about letting go
and opening up
I have written about
the wisdom of cats
the symphony of nature
about the mute display
of flowers in my garden
I have written poems
about food
and floods
and the courage
of refugees

I need to write this poem
one last poem
in a long cycle
and I am searching for words
searching for meaning
searching for hope

and I look into the mirror
of your face

your kind face
your wise face
your forever face
and I am listening to your voice
your sweet aging and sageing voice
and I take to heart
I have seen you
and heard you
through the ages
and your echo is profound
infinite and infinitely healing

I know when I lay me down
and go to sleep
I may awaken
and one of our voices
has been silenced
I may not embrace you again
maybe I have crossed the bridge
or maybe you
and I know that in the freedom
that awaits us
when our bodies have let go
our embrace
is infinite
we will always love each other
there is such peace in my soul
such peace in my soul
we will always love each other
we will always love each other

neither of us has to say amen
we are each other's amen
amen   amen   amen